IN SEARCH OF BRAVER ANGELS

Getting Along Together in Troubled Times

By David Blankenhorn

Braver Angels
733 Third Avenue, 16th Floor
New York, NY 10017

ISBN 978-0-578-99630-1

David Blankenhorn

USA Today describes David Blankenhorn as "a catalyst for analysis and debate among those with differing views." The *Deseret News* says he has "carved out a unique career cutting across ideological lines." He is co-founder and president of Braver Angels, a citizens' organization working for less rancor and more goodwill in American politics and society. He also founded the Institute for American Values, a think tank focusing on civil society, co-founded the National Fatherhood Initiative, and in high school founded the Mississippi Community Service Corps and the Virginia Community Service Corps. He's written or co-edited 14 books. He grew up in Jackson, Mississippi, graduated from Harvard College, and received an M.A. in history from the University of Warwick in Coventry, England. He lives in New York City.

Praise for *In Search of Braver Angels*

David Blankenhorn is a national treasure. As a civic organizer, a thought leader, a sometimes controversial advocate, and now a conciliator, he has shown how passionate conviction and loving civility can coexist. Now, in his wise, engaging, and eminently practical collection of essays, he shows us all how we, and the country we love, can reclaim our better selves.

—Jonathan Rauch, Brookings Institution, author of *The Constitution of Knowledge*

Immerse yourself in this book. David Blankenhorn expertly offers the solutions for rebuilding trust between our citizens.

—Tim Roemer, Co-Chair of Issue One, former U.S. Member of Congress, 9/11 Commissioner, and Ambassador to India

We can never be afraid to talk to the other side, and David Blankenhorn is helping us do that. This book is full of wisdom for anyone working to build a more just America.

—Hawk Newsome, Black Lives Matter

How can people so divided by politics ever hope to work together? Drawing on his life's work of bringing political opponents together face-to-face, David Blankenhorn points us toward dialogue, trust, and a collective reckoning of who we are as a people.

—Samara Klar, University of Arizona, co-author of *Independent Politics*

Braver Angels was a great idea when David Blankenhorn helped found it in 2016. Five years later, it has become a national treasure in our politically impoverished nation. This book contains Blankenhorn's most insightful and inspiring essays from this challenging period.

—Jonathan Haidt, New York University, author of *The Righteous Mind*

Dedicated to the leaders and members of Braver Angels

Table of Contents

Introduction

This book is haunted by a question and a person.

The question is fundamental. Can our American experiment in ordered liberty survive our current afflictions of vanishing social trust and escalating political rancor? I worry that it cannot and believe that our great task is to see that it does. Every page of this book—whether on how liberals and conservatives talk past each other, how convenience stores and road signs reveal us, or the roots of social conflict—is devoted to answering this question and depicting this task.

The person haunting this book is Abraham Lincoln. Lincoln was president during the most horrible moments of mistrust and rancor in American history. He was an imperfect man, and he and his generation failed to prevent disunion and civil war. But for me, Lincoln's successes and failures, and most of all his temperament, are inexhaustible opportunities for learning, even more so as we Americans today face our own time of testing. He was my constant companion in writing this book.

WHAT'S MORE IMPORTANT THAN WHO WINS?

Democracy is government by talk. The goal is to keep the conversation going, even when doing so seems pointless, too painful to bear, or likely to produce outcomes that many view as intolerable. There are alternatives to government by talk, but no democratic alternatives.

Democracy is also government by adjustment. In democracies, differences are typically settled by compromises that leave both sides dissatisfied. No victory is total, no answer is final, rarely does either side vanquish the other. There are alternatives to government by adjustment, but all of them involve exclusion and coercion.

Regardless of which side won or is about to win any particular election, America's fundamental choice today is whether we will govern ourselves going forward by talk and adjustment, or whether we have come to view our differences as so entrenched, and so intractable, that the only way forward is to separate into self-reinforcing groups that not only disagree with each other, but also view each other as enemies.

What do Americans today think about this choice? Two fascinating numbers shed some light. A poll conducted in October 2020, just weeks before the presidential election, found that about 70 percent of both Republicans and Democrats either strongly agreed or agreed that "If the wrong candidate wins this election, America will not recover."

At the same time, about 70 percent of Americans from both parties either strongly agreed or agreed that "After the election, the two sides working together is more important than the winning side getting its way."

These apparently contradictory findings point to the heart of our current crisis.

First, most voters in both parties believe that America is seriously threatened by bad actors. Most of us even view this risk as close to existential: If the wrong side wins the next election, "America will not recover." In such dire circumstances, should I compromise with what I view as an ultimate danger? Should I seek to reach understandings and split differences with those who would cripple, perhaps permanently, the America I know and love? Surely a plausible and morally defensible answer to these questions is "no."

In fact, we see this "no" all around us today. A progressive friend tells me that, as an African American, he has no interest in seeking common ground with people whose views literally threaten his life. A conservative friend tells me that it's worse than pointless to seek accommodations with people who would take away basic American freedoms. Growing numbers on both sides argue that, since the other side has the upper hand when it comes to raw power, conversation itself is a rigged process that almost never produces fair outcomes.

If we look to elected officials and candidates, the "no" is the same, only louder. Bad faith on the other side is assumed. Empathy is viewed as weakness, compromise as capitulation. By far the most popular word on both sides, when appealing to voters, is "fight." Apparently millions of voters favor this kind of politician, making this kind of appeal.

Yet on a second and quite different note, about 70 percent of us in each party also say that our main priority, even more important than the good side prevailing, should be the two sides working together. Almost by definition, such a shift in our political culture would require all of us to demonstrate much more conciliation, much more self-restraint, and a much greater willingness to compromise, even on issues involving first principles. This is what most Democrats and most Republicans want.

Really? Surely the argument against this position is a strong one, especially in these times. In fact, could any political stance be viewed as more self-defeating and cowardly, particularly when both sides are also convinced that their adversaries willfully seek to inflict wounds from which America will not recover?

Here we see the nub of our dilemma. We're implicated individually and socially in what can feel like irresolvable contradictions. We expect evil from our opponents, yet we want to cooperate with them. We fundamentally mistrust the other side, yet we want to be trustworthy, even as we know that trust exists only if it's reciprocal. We view certain things as non-negotiable, yet we want to be willing to negotiate.

In one of Samuel Beckett's novels, a character says, "I can't go on. I'll go on." Can both things even be possible? In a 2020 interview, the novelist Marilyn Robinson says that "it's a huge concession" for her to say that she'll consider discussing political outcomes that she views as unacceptable, yet "we have to be able to talk to each other or we've lost the whole thing." By "the whole thing," she means our democracy. In the name of justice she recoils from going on, but in the name of democracy she'll go on. Let none of us underestimate how hard this is.

Besides talk and adjustment, democracy also seems to require government by faith. Especially in times of crisis, democracy may require us to believe in things currently unseen—things such as magnanimity, trust, empathy, and the confidence that we can lessen our differences enough to live together in comity.

Most Americans in both parties retain that faith. Despite the rancor, and recognizing the dangers, we want to keep the conversation going. The great task before us is to discover how.

TWO CURES FOR POLITICAL RANCOR

Rancor in our politics is like the weather. It's everywhere. Also like the weather, as Mark Twain said, everybody talks about it, but nobody does anything about it.

That can change. We could reshape American politics now by adopting two simple rules, each named after the American president who wrote it.

The Eisenhower Rule says: "Reserve criticism for private conference. Speak only good in public." Dwight David Eisenhower followed this rule his entire public life, which helps explain why he was one of the last U.S. presidents widely admired by both Republicans and Democrats. Ike had many critics whose policies he publicly and vigorously opposed and to whom he spoke bluntly in private, but he never publicly attacked an adversary. In public, he spoke only good of others.

The Lincoln Rule says: "If you would win a person to your cause, first convince them that you are their sincere friend." Abraham Lincoln probably endured more public abuse than any other leader of his generation. But he typically treated even his harshest critics with tolerance and charity. He knew that argument without kindness rarely works and that warm engagement is far more persuasive than correct instruction.

No public attacks. Start with friendship. Following these simple rules would make everything better. Would the sun shine brighter? Would all rainy days produce rainbows? Well, maybe not. But almost! Consider just a few of the wonderful benefits we'd enjoy.

Our entire media world would be turned inside out. TV news organizations that abandoned political goodwill long ago would either change course or face financial ruin. Our most famous commentators would either transform their on-air personalities or be rendered speechless. How great would that be?

Disallowing unkind attacks in our print media would reduce total print output dramatically, thus not only saving our sanity and many journalists' souls, but also saving many trees from being pulped into paper. In fact, under the new rules, much political journalism as currently practiced would simply disappear, causing many new jobs and opportunities to open up for those bold enough to try something more respectable.

The worst features of social media would disappear. Political talk on Facebook and Twitter would self-decontaminate. People who leave snarky, mean-spirited comments under everything they read would no longer feel free to do so, which would largely eliminate online commenting. Are you feeling the possibilities here?

But there's more. We'd become better individuals. The millions of hours we now devote to bad-mouthing each other over politics would suddenly free up. Think of all those reclaimed hours to fill with genuine pleasures!

Let's talk about manners. Our wisest authorities on the subject teach us that good manners are less about knowing which fork to use than about knowing when and how to practice self-restraint in consideration of others. The goal of minding your manners isn't good form, but a better heart.

That's why our two rules could usher in a golden age of good manners. We'd continue to disagree, often strongly, and sometimes over first principles, but publicly ridiculing those with whom we disagree would no longer signal one's virtue. We might not feel friendly toward our opponents, but we'd at least need to pretend that we do. Feigned decency in political conduct would be the new tax that vice pays to virtue. And who knows? As we fake it, we might begin to make it.

Let's talk about our health. Would less malice in our political debate mean fewer strokes and heart attacks linked to high blood pressure, chronic stress, and debilitating anger? Would treating each other with more respect produce citizens with more resilience, less down-heartedness and depression, and fewer feelings of alienation and isolation? Perhaps. We might discover that political decency is also a public health measure.

I'm confident that we'd be spiritually healthier. We'd wash off a thick coating of ethical slime to which we've tragically become accustomed. We'd feel morally cleaner, like happy children in fresh clothes. We'd rediscover the teaching of the Scriptures: "A kind answer turns away wrath."

What's holding us back from what we need so much? Courage. Courage is arguably the chief virtue, because it gives us strength to live out the other virtues, even when doing so appears naïve or likely to invite ridicule. Today in the United States, a bit of courage is all we need to find what Lincoln called the better angels of our nature.

THREE APPROACHES TO CONFLICT

Social conflict is when groups struggle against each other over social goals or arrangements. I'm engaged in social conflict when my group attempts to resist, oppose, or coerce the will of others. Social conflict is a core feature of modern societies and appears to be a universal or near-universal feature of human groups.

Social conflict can take many forms. Some forms (such as sullen silence) are tacit, while other forms (from verbal debate to organized warfare) are open and explicit.

Conflict is related to competition, but the two are not the same. Competition becomes conflict only when the attention of the competitors is diverted from the objects of competition to each other. Social conflict, then, is when my group seeks to achieve its goals at least in part by preventing other groups from achieving theirs.

Many great thinkers have tried to identify the fundamental sources of social conflict. Saint Augustine, the early Christian writer, traced social conflict to *libido dominandi*, or the lust to dominate others. The 17th-century political philosopher Thomas Hobbes traced it to man's innate desire to "do as he pleases." Hobbes' fellow philosopher John Locke traced it to humankind's limited capacity for generosity. The great 19th-century student of American democracy Alexis de Tocqueville pointed to the diminished influence in society of what he called "self-interest rightly understood," by which he meant the understanding that, in general, what's good for others is also good for me and mine. Marxists and other writers have emphasized the role of competition for scarce or valuable economic resources. According to many writers, an important engine of social conflict in modern societies is clashing moral values, or strong disagreements over what is good and how we should treat one another.

Is social conflict a blessing or a curse? On the one hand, we could stipulate a moral continuum, with cooperation (the best) on one end of the continuum and conflict (the worst) on the other. In this way of thinking, conflict is clearly something we should be against—the more of it we have, the worse off we become.

Another and likely fuller understanding is that social conflict is not only a universal occurrence in human societies, but is also frequently a healthy and at times necessary occurrence. After all, in many cases social progress is impossible without social conflict. Probably the most important question about social conflict, then, is not whether it exists (it does), or whether we can eliminate it (we can't), or even whether we should *try* to eliminate it (we shouldn't). The real question is *how we should approach it.*

Our national motto, *E pluribus unum*, means "from many, one." It tells us that people from many and often conflicting backgrounds and views can live on this continent in conditions of unprecedented freedom while also thriving together as one people. It tells us neither to deny nor to inflame our differences, but instead to seek to reconcile them at higher levels in order to form what our Constitution calls "a more perfect Union."

Implicit in our national motto—implicit in the founders' vision—is a theory of conflict. It seems that there are three basic approaches to conflict, which we can also think of as three stages, from simplest and worst to hardest and best.

1. Submit

In the first approach or stage, we submit to conflict. Conflict is in charge. Some people in this stage ignore conflict, failing to acknowledge that it exists. Others internalize conflict and thus make conflict their cause, becoming both its relentless advocate as well as its captive. Either way, polarization is perpetuated, as conflict dominates society rather than the other way around.

> *I am aware that many object to the severity of my language; but is there not cause for severity? I will be as harsh as Truth, and as uncompromising as Justice. On this subject I do not wish to think, or speak, or write, with moderation. No! No! Tell a man whose house is on fire to give a moderate alarm; tell him to moderately rescue his wife from the hands of the ravisher; tell the mother to gradually extricate her babe from the fire into which it has fallen—but urge me not to use moderation in a cause like the present. I am in earnest—I will not equivocate—I will not excuse—I will not retreat a single inch—and I will be heard.*
>
> —William Lloyd Garrison, *The Liberator*, 1831

2. Manage

A second approach is when we seek to clarify and manage conflict. By trying to assume good faith in our adversaries and trying to correct partial understandings and false stereotypes, we aim in this stage to achieve actual rather than inflated or imagined disagreement. This better and more difficult approach to dealing with conflict requires both civility in our treatment of one another and a willingness to acknowledge areas of common ground. At least as importantly, insofar as we want conflict not only clarified but also managed for the good of society, this approach also requires the capacity for negotiation, compromise, and mutual accommodation.

> *When a broad table is to be made, and the edges of planks do not fit, the artist takes a little from both, and makes a good joint. In like manner, here, both sides must part from some of their demands, in order that they may join in some accommodating proposition.*
>
> —Benjamin Franklin, Constitutional Convention, 1787

3. Transform

A third approach is when we seek to transform conflict. In this approach, we do not avoid or deny conflict. Nor do we become its pliant servant and enabler. Nor do we stop and declare victory once we have understood conflict accurately by using the tools of reason and empathy and managed it pragmatically by using the tools of compromise. In this hardest and yet arguably most fruitful way of dealing with conflict, we try to go beyond polarization and beyond compromise, toward a creative new framing—a higher synthesis—that includes what is valid and helpful on both sides, leading us, together, to a new place in the discussion. This approach depends significantly on epistemological humility, recognizing relationship-building as a valid shaper of identity and viewpoint, and a belief in the equal dignity of every person.

> *When conflict arises, some people simply look at it and go their way as if nothing happened; they wash their hands of it and get on with their lives. Others embrace it in such a way that they become its prisoners; they lose their bearings, project onto institutions their own confusion and dissatisfaction and thus make unity impossible. But there is also a third way, and it is the best way to deal with conflict. It is the willingness to face conflict head on, to resolve it and to make it a link in the chain of a new process.*
>
> *In this way it becomes possible to build communion amid disagreement, but this can only be achieved by those great persons who are willing to go beyond the surface of the conflict and to see others in their deepest dignity. This requires acknowledging a principle indispensable to the building of friendship in society: namely, that unity is greater than conflict. Solidarity, in its deepest and most challenging*

> *sense, thus becomes a way of making history in a life setting where conflicts, tensions, and oppositions can achieve a diversified and life-giving unity. This is not to opt for a kind of syncretism, or for the absorption of one into the other, but rather for a resolution which takes place on a higher plane and preserves what is valid and useful on both sides.*
>
> —Pope Francis, *Evangelii Gaudium*, 2014

The founders feared that the first approach to conflict would destroy the nation. (In 1861-65, it almost did.) They ordained and established the U.S. Constitution to embody the second approach. And they left us many words and deeds, including the ideal of *E pluribus unum*, to help us aspire to the third approach.

Figure 1. Hierarchy of Approaches to Conflict

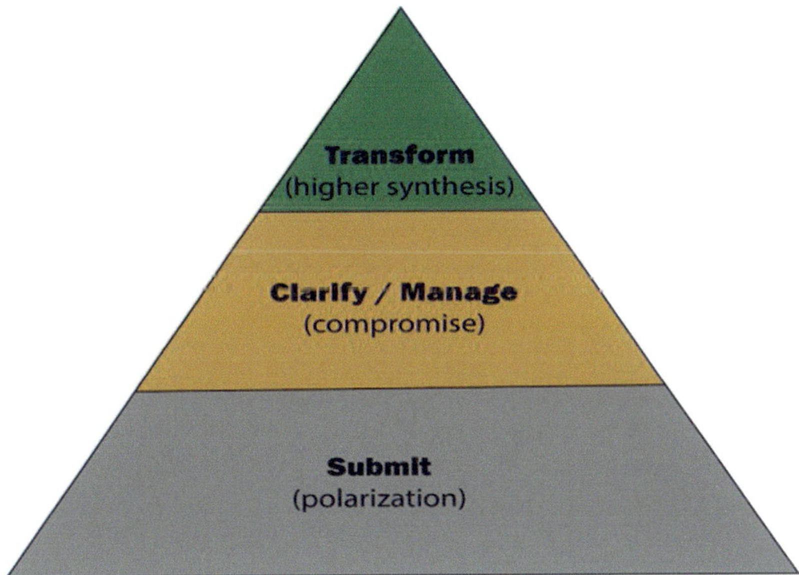

Figure 2. By Nicky Case

SEVEN HABITS OF HIGHLY DEPOLARIZING PEOPLE

In recent decades, we Americans have become highly practiced in the skills and mental habits of demonizing our political opponents. All our metrics agree that we currently do political polarization *very* well, and researchers tell us that we're getting better at it all the time.

For example, Stanford Professor Shanto Iyengar and his colleagues recently found that when it comes both to trusting other people with your money and evaluating applications of high school seniors, Americans today are less friendly to people in the other political party than they are to people of a different race. The researchers conclude that "Americans increasingly dislike people and groups on the other side of the political divide and face no social repercussions for the open expression of these attitudes." As a result, today "the level of partisan animus in the American public exceeds racial animus." That's saying something!

But if polarization is all around us, familiar as an old coat, what about its opposite? What would depolarization look and sound like? Would we know it if we saw it, in others or in ourselves? Perhaps most importantly, what are the mental habits that encourage it?

We're confronted with an irony here. We Americans didn't necessarily think our way into political polarization, but we'll likely have to think our way out. A number of big structural and social trends—including the end of the Cold War, the rising importance of cultural issues in our politics, growing secularization, greater racial and ethnic diversity, the shift from the Greatest Generation to Baby Boomers as the nation's dominant elites, the breakup of the old-media system, the increasing ideological coherence of both of our two main political parties, among others—appear to have helped produce our current predicament.

Yet over time, the intellectual habits encouraged by these underlying shifts developed a life and autonomy of their own. They became "baked in," ultimately forming a new popular wisdom regarding how we judge what is true and decide what is right in public life. The intellectual habits of polarization include binary (Manichaean) thinking, absolutizing one's preferred values, viewing uncertainty as a weakness, privileging deductive thinking, assuming that one's opponents are motivated by bad faith, and hesitating to agree on basic facts and the meaning of evidence.

What are the antidotes to these familiar habits? We can recognize the mindset of the polarizer, but how does the depolarizer understand conflict and try to make sense of the world? Here is an attempt to answer these questions, by way of proposing the seven habits of highly depolarizing people.

1. Criticize from within.

In other words, criticize the other—whether person, group, or society—on the basis of something you have in common. The political philosopher Michael Walzer describes this approach as "internal criticism." He writes: "We criticize our society just as we criticize our friends, on the assumption that the terms of the critique, the moral references, are common." As Walzer and many others have observed, besides being depolarizing, criticizing from within is typically much more effective than criticizing from outside.

This idea of recognizing something that is shared with the other—even in moments of fierce conflict—is beautifully reflected in Lincoln's use of the term "better angels" in his First Inaugural Address, on the eve of the Civil War. William Seward, who would serve as Secretary of State under Lincoln, had suggested that the new president conclude by calling on "the guardian angel of the nation." Lincoln changed it to "the better angels of our nature." In Seward's version, what was needed would come from outside us. In Lincoln's version, it would come from within us, something "better" in the "nature" of both Northerners and Southerners.

2. Look for goods in conflict.

Some conflicts are entirely about good versus evil or right versus wrong, but many (probably most) are more about good versus good or right versus right. Each side, at least in part, is likely to be defending a goal or value that both recognize as worthy. Political philosophers such as Isaiah Berlin and William Galston have referred to this type of disagreement as one of "goods in conflict." The challenge in such cases is to recognize and weigh competing goods—a challenge that is different from (and may be harder than) distinguishing good from bad. Looking always for the possible existence of goods in conflict not only contributes to depolarization, it also contributes to achieving valid (as opposed to phony) disagreement.

3. Count higher than two.

Of all the mental habits that encourage polarization, the most dangerous is probably binary thinking—the tendency to divide everything into two mutually antagonistic categories. Sometimes an important phenomenon actually *does* divide naturally into two and only two parts or sides, between which one all-or-nothing choice must be made. But in most cases, this way of thinking about the world is not only polarizing, it is highly simplistic and leads mainly to pseudo-disagreements as opposed to real ones. One may be the loneliest number, but in the area of social criticism and conflict, two is probably the most harmful. In thinking through any challenge or conflict, the highly depolarizing person's first question is, "Can I count higher than two?"

4. Doubt.

Doubt—the concern that my views may not be entirely correct—is the true friend of wisdom and (along with empathy, to which it's related) the greatest enemy of polarization. The playwright and political leader Václav Havel famously said that he would rather have a beer with someone who's searching for the truth than with someone who's found it. Now, Havel was a man of the firmest convictions. He went to jail for them and helped to start a revolution on behalf of them. So he was certainly not advocating, even in jest, a way of thinking that leads to passivity or an inability to choose; quite the opposite. He was advocating against the type of certitude that breeds smugness and contempt for one's opponents, and which gradually transforms the natural appetite for empathetic engagement and the free play of intellect into an appetite for lecturing and pointing out to others the error of their ways. In today's polarized environment, doubt is often treated as a weakness or even a sin (as is its cousin, changing one's mind). But the opposite is more likely to be true. Doubt often supports true convictions based on realistic foundations, just as doubtlessness is nearly always an intellectual disability, a form of blindness.

In his Second Inaugural Address in 1865, as the Civil War neared its end, Abraham Lincoln could have declared his certainty that God favored his side. But in one of the most important statements ever uttered by a U.S. president, Lincoln, who could lead a war and sacrifice his life for his convictions while remaining deeply empathetic, said simply: "The Almighty has His own purposes."

5. Specify.

Because generalization is both an ally and a frequent indicator of polarization, highly depolarizing people tend to be connoisseurs of the specific. This dedication to specificity can express itself in at least four important ways.

The first way is a persistent skepticism about categories. Of course, categories and the process of categorization are essential to human thought and expression; we can't do without them. But all categories are abstractions, and when we turn the healthy need to categorize into the sloppy habit of categorical thinking—applying abstract labels (such as the political labels "Left" and "Right")—to everything and everyone on the grounds that we have accurately separated them into non-overlapping categories, the result is personally and socially harmful.

It's also worth remembering that, in many cases, creative and categorical thinking are at odds with each other. American musical innovators from Louis Armstrong to Charlie Parker to Bob Dylan have been famously indifferent and even hostile to musical categories: Armstrong said that the only two kinds of music are what you like and what you don't; Dylan, booed while onstage in London for not singing "folk" music, memorably told the audience that he cared about "American music." The same is true of many of our most creative scholars, including the noted mid-20th-century sociologist David Riesman and the prominent political philosopher Jean Bethke Elshtain, neither of whom was content for a moment to stay within a single disciplinary box or intellectual category.

A second way to favor specificity is to consider each issue separately and on its own terms, as opposed to assuming the validity of a governing ideological framework, such as "conservatism" or "liberalism." Indeed, in his seminal discussion of "the trap of ideology," the great sociologist Daniel Bell tells us:

> *The point is that ideologists are "terrible simplifiers." Ideology makes it unnecessary for people to confront individual issues on their own merits. One simply turns to the ideological vending machine, and then the prepared formulae. And when these ideas are suffused with apocalyptic fervor, ideas become weapons, with dreadful results.*

A third way to specify is to privilege the specific assertion (including the empirically valid generalization) over the general assertion. As Jonathan Rauch observes, a turning point in the development of modern science was the discovery—in geology around the turn of the 19th century, and soon recognized by other fields—that shifting the argument *away* from abstract and often philosophically charged questions ("Can miracles be invoked to explain natural phenomena?") and *toward* specific empirical questions ("Are fossils found in the same order throughout the Devonian shale?") can help to defuse paralyzing controversies and even turn ideological foes into fellow researchers. Scientists can be as stubborn and ideological as anyone else, of course, but the field's focus on specificity and empirical inquiry ("Show me!") has done much to foster more constructive conversations.

The fourth way to favor specificity is to rely first and foremost on inductive reasoning, which tries to build conclusions from the bottom up by accumulating specific data points, as compared to deductive reasoning, which tries to build conclusions from the top down by exploring the implications of true general premises or statements. Deduction is the great friend of ideology (especially "total ideology"). Induction specifies.

6. Qualify (in most cases).

To qualify something you say is to make it less definitive, less comprehensive, and more nuanced, and thus to acknowledge the possibility that some pieces of the puzzle may still be missing. To qualify, then, is almost always to announce—even if indirectly—a willingness to engage further with the other side in pursuit of getting it right. Another meaning of "to qualify" is to enumerate the qualities or characteristics of something. In this sense, the habit of qualifying is cousin to the habit of specifying.

A third meaning is to be or become competent for a task or position. (As in: "She's qualified for the job.") The act of qualifying, then, is broadly associated with the condition of being duly prepared. In this sense, we might suggest that persons who "do not qualify"—either in the sense of lacking needed credentials *or* in the sense of making claims without duly qualifying them—are likely neither fully competent nor ready to fulfill the requirements of office or trust.

Of course, in today's world of dueling talking points and partisan political warfare, qualifying—in the sense of modifying or limiting, often by giving exceptions—is frequently treated as a sign of insufficient zeal and perhaps even of wimpiness. But for the serious mind, the opposite is true. To qualify is to demonstrate competence. And for the highly depolarizing person, to err is human; to qualify, divine.

7. Keep the conversation going.

At the very heart of democratic civil society is the idea that we don't stop talking to one another, even when—perhaps especially when—the conversation is frustrating and seems futile. Why? Because ending the conversation is tantamount to ending the relationship, and when the relationship ends, everything hardens, polarization reigns, and your opponents turn into your enemies. When we end a conversation, we typically fill the void with accusations, name-calling, exaggeration, and the striking of poses.

Keeping the conversation going is itself a style of conversation, and even a way of thinking. The political philosopher Jean Bethke Elshtain reminds us that "a commitment to democratic politics, or the possibility of such a politics, commits one to an imperative to keep debates alive rather than attempting to resolve them definitively by silencing one side to a dispute . . ." In her own work, therefore, she strives to "articulate a strong set of claims that do not have the effect of silencing the voices of others." She writes:

"The need for, or conviction of, a correct and encompassing standpoint, the immediate excitement and visceral satisfaction of theories that make possible scenarios in which the analyst moves in on a given turf, sets up court, and summarily dispenses epistemic and political 'justice,' is one I eschew and devoutly hope that I avoid."

The concept of "Seven Habits of Highly Depolarizing People" draws inspiration from two sources. The first, of course, is Stephen R. Covey's outstanding book *The 7 Habits of Highly Effective People.* The second is the seven virtues of classical Christianity. Moreover, just as those seven virtues are divided by teachers into two categories—the so-called theological or transcendent virtues of faith, hope, and charity; and the so-called cardinal or natural virtues of prudence, justice, fortitude, and temperance—the seven habits of highly depolarizing people can also be divided into two categories, with habits one through three (criticize from within, look for goods in conflict, count higher than two) being the highest habits, or those of the most overarching importance, and four through seven (doubt, specify, qualify, and keep the conversation going) being the cardinal habits, or those attainable intellectual habits on which so much else depends.

Will they work? They do for me. I have my own wounds from the culture wars, as many of us do, and some of mine have been self-inflicted. As I've attempted recently to transition to less-polarizing ways of analyzing issues and expressing myself, I've found that it helps to keep these seven habits in mind, in the hope that they'll eventually become my intellectual default settings.

Making use of them certainly doesn't tell me *what* to think about any particular issue, but attending to them does seem to help me think more carefully and, I hope, more honestly. Ultimately, habits of mind oriented to depolarization are, to change metaphors again, less a microscope than a new pair of glasses—less a way of seeing a few things more clearly than a different way of seeing many things. And surely a different way of seeing is what's needed. As Lincoln put it in 1862, when "the occasion is piled high with difficulty," the first and great challenge is to "think anew."

TEN WAYS TO DEFUSE POLITICAL ARROGANCE

The warm glow of being certain that my political views are correct. The thrill of the perfectly formulated gotcha question. The combined feelings of fury and astonishment that my political adversaries could be so stupid, so evil, so misguided. Welcome to our era. We live in the age of arrogance—an unforgiving, intolerant, anger-stoked age of entrenched confirmation bias across groups and of constantly alleged binary political choices in which your position is entirely wrong and mine is entirely right.

This way of understanding those with whom we disagree has become so prevalent that we may come to view it as normal, or inevitable, though it's neither. Nor is this tumor benign. Believing that my political opponents are either deluded or trying to cause harm destroys the trust on which civil society depends. It wrecks politics and political discussion. It weakens our intellects. It distorts the mission of higher education. It threatens family life. It ends friendships.

What is to be done? The ultimate antidote for political arrogance is political humility, which is a branch of intellectual humility. And so I rise with soft clear voice to sing its praises.

Intellectual humility appears to be a malleable personality trait. We can define it briefly as the capacity for recognizing that a particular personal belief or position may be fallible. Accordingly, intellectually humble people typically understand their own beliefs as subject to further consideration and typically feel willing and able to learn from the views of others, even those with whom they strongly disagree.

For centuries, intellectual humility was understood as a character virtue to be cultivated. Socrates, a founder of Western philosophy, embodied and taught it in classical Athens. In "Enquiry Concerning Human Understanding," from 1748, the Scottish philosopher David Hume expresses one of his principal conclusions this way: "In general, there is a degree of doubt, and caution, and modesty, which, in all kinds of scrutiny and decision, ought for ever to accompany a just reasoner." Benjamin Franklin, in his warnings about the self-defeating qualities of "dogmatical expression," describes intellectual humility as one of society's most useful virtues.

At the personal level, intellectual humility counterbalances narcissism, self-centeredness, pridefulness, and the need to dominate others. Conversely, intellectual humility seems to correlate positively with empathy, responsiveness to reasons, the ability to acknowledge what one owes (including intellectually) to others, and the moral capacity for equal regard of others. Arguably its ultimate fruit is a more accurate understanding of oneself and one's capacities. Intellectual humility also appears frequently to correlate positively with successful leadership (due especially to the link between intellectual humility and trustworthiness) and with rightly earned self-confidence.

At the social and political levels, intellectual humility is a primary democratic virtue. Many political philosophers across the centuries have insisted on its importance. Why? Because, as the political philosopher Jean Bethke Elshtain has put it, "a responsible politics is one that appreciates the limits to our understanding: we don't know enough and can, in principle, never know enough to advance epistemological and political certitude."

Indeed, without those habits and commitments associated with intellectual humility—dialogue based on reason-giving, openness to other views, rational argument in the service of truth, and norms of forbearance, civility, and self-restraint—democracy itself is poisoned and can grind to a halt. For this reason, intellectual humility may be *the* essential cure for the condemn-your-neighbor political polarization now dominating our society.

Analytically, and especially when considered as a character virtue, we can view intellectual humility as a wisely discerned middle ground (the golden mean) between the two extremes of intellectual arrogance and intellectual servility.

Viewed this way, intellectual humility can, but does not need to, lead to the inability to act with courage and conviction. Abraham Lincoln gave his life for the preservation of the Union. Martin Luther King, Jr., gave his for the beloved community. The Czech playwright and political leader Václav Havel showed matchless fortitude in the fight against authoritarianism.

Yet these three are among my heroes in large measure because of their intellectual humility. For their highest principles they risked all, but they were never ideologues. They never bragged, never gloated, never considered the conversation closed. They never suggested in word or deed that doubt is the enemy of truth or that humility undermines conviction.

We can similarly view intellectual humility as the wisest balance between, on the one hand, the belief that truth exists and is objective, and on the other, the knowledge that our access to the truth is subjective and therefore partial. Understanding this balance suggests that the search for the truth we revere is best undertaken in recognition of our limitations and in collaboration with others.

As noted earlier, Havel once said that he would rather have a beer with someone searching for the truth than with someone who has found it. An important quality of both scientific inquiry and democratic political discourse is the understanding that all can learn from all and that important conversations don't end.

Finally, intellectual humility is not a free-standing (purely heritable) or fixed human quality. It's like baseball. It can be done well or badly, and doing it well requires practice and repetition. Nor does excellence typically arise only from internal effort. Like baseball, intellectual humility is most proficiently played as a team sport.

Accordingly, my capacity for intellectual humility depends importantly on a surrounding culture that prizes it and expects it, particularly of its leaders, that institutionalizes it, and that teaches it, especially to the young.

A number of societal conditions are favorable to cultivating intellectual humility. They include:

- Knowing conceptually what intellectual humility is and how to recognize it in others;
- Participating in institutions that value openness and flexibility and that tolerate and often welcome uncertainty;
- Receiving environment feedback that permits us to understand accurately what we do and do not know;
- Being exposed to the benefits of intellectual humility, such as improved decision-making, better relationships with others, and enhanced organizational and social progress; and
- Being exposed to societal leaders who model intellectual humility, are admired by others because of it, and whose success is in part attributed to it.

What can be done to help produce these conditions? Here are 10 ideas.

Education:

1. Encourage social scientists to conceptualize and measure intellectual humility. (This is already beginning to happen.)
2. Teach children in family, community, and religious life that consciously cultivating intellectual humility is a way to become both a smart person (with a high "Civic IQ") and a good person.
3. Promote intellectual humility on college campuses as a gateway to knowledge and an antidote to politicized higher education.

Politics and Media:

4. Seek the revival of "regular order" (rules and customs intended to produce deliberation and compromise) in the U.S. Congress.
5. Seek the revival of senatorial courtesy in the U.S. Senate. (The principle here is that attitudes follow behavior. If I dislike you, but must pretend otherwise in my external behavior because custom obliges me to use prescribed language indicating respect, I may eventually come to suspect that you deserve respect. Thus *acting as if* I respect you can increase my respect.)
6. Replace posturing and publicity-seeking with actual give-and-take communication in town hall meetings with members of Congress.
7. Encourage (mild-mannered) arrogance-shaming of those in the public eye acting with gross intellectual arrogance.
8. Create and seek to make popular a social media code of ethics.

Community Life:

9. Do everything we can to foster social class and racial integration.
10. Create more opportunities for citizens to talk with (not just at) one another across partisan divides.

Will any of this work? Of course it will. My logic is flawless and my argument is irresistible. And if you can't see that, you are a bad person who doesn't care about others. Of this I'm certain.

FOURTEEN CAUSES OF POLARIZATION

Why do Americans increasingly believe that those in the other party are not only misguided but are also bad people whose views are so dangerously wrongheaded and crazy as to be all but incomprehensible? What has created what Arthur Brooks in his book *Love Your Enemies* calls a "culture of contempt" in American politics and public life?

I'm glad you asked! Behold a baker's dozen worth of causes.

1. The end of the Cold War. The West's victory in the Cold War means that (with the possible exception of jihadi terrorism) there is no longer a global enemy to keep us united as we focus on a powerful and cohesive external threat.

2. The rise of identity-group politics. On both the Left and the Right, the main conceptual frameworks have largely shifted in focus from unifying values to group identities. As Amy Chua puts it in *Political Tribes* (2018): "The Left believes that right-wing tribalism—bigotry, racism—is tearing the country apart. The Right believes that left-wing tribalism—identity politics, political correctness—is tearing the country apart. They are both right." (Never mind here the problematic usage of the terms "tribe" and "tribal.")

3. Growing religious diversity. Current trends in American religion reflect as well as contribute to political polarization. One trend is growing secularization, including a declining share of Americans who are Christians, less public confidence in organized religion, and rising numbers of religiously unaffiliated Americans. One consequence is an increasingly open contestation of Christianity's once-dominant role in American public and political culture. But another trend is the continuing, and in some respects intensifying, robustness of religious faith and practice in many parts of the society. This growing religious divide helps to explain the rise of several of the most polarizing social issues in our politics, such as LGBTQ issues, religious freedom, and abortion. It also contributes to polarizing the two political parties overall, as religious belief becomes an increasingly important predictor of party affiliation. For example, among Democrats and Democratic-leaning U.S. adults, religiously unaffiliated voters (the "nones") are now more numerous than Catholics, evangelical Protestants, mainline Protestants, or members of historically black Protestant traditions, whereas socially and theologically conservative Christians today are overwhelmingly Republican.

4. *Growing racial and ethnic diversity*. In the long run, increased racial and ethnic diversity is likely a strength. But in the short run—which means now—it contributes to a decline in social trust (the belief that we can understand and count on one another) and a rise in social and political conflict.

5. *The passing of the Greatest Generation*. We don't call them the greatest for no reason. Their generational values, forged in the trials of the Great Depression and World War II—including a willingness to sacrifice for country, concern for the general welfare, a mature character structure, and adherence to a shared civic faith—reduced social and political polarization. Thus, note:

> *I didn't vote for him but he's my President, and I hope he does a good job.*
>
> —John Wayne (b. 1907) on the election of John F. Kennedy in 1960

> *I hope he fails.*
>
> —Rush Limbaugh (b. 1951) on the election of Barack Obama in 2008

6. *Geographical sorting*. Americans today are increasingly living in politically like-minded communities. Living only or mainly with like-minded neighbors makes us both more extreme and more certain in our political beliefs. As Bill Bishop and Robert Cushing put it in *The Big Sort* (2008): "Mixed company moderates; like-minded company polarizes. Heterogeneous communities restrain group excesses; homogeneous communities march toward the extremes."

Percent of U.S. voters living in counties in which a presidential candidate won by a "landslide" margin of 20 percent or more of the vote:

1976: 25
2016: 60

7. *Political party sorting*. Once upon a time, there were such creatures as liberal Republicans and conservative Democrats. No longer. The parties have sorted philosophically such that today almost all liberals are Democrats and nearly all conservatives are Republicans. One main result is that the partisan gap between the parties is wide and getting wider.

> *Across 10 measures that Pew Research Center has tracked on the same surveys since 1994, the average partisan gap has increased from 15 percentage points to 36 points.*
>
> —Pew Research Center, 2017

8. *New rules for Congress*. The weakening and in some cases elimination of "regular order"—defined broadly as the rules,

customs, and precedents intended to promote orderly and deliberative policymaking—as well as the erosion of traditions such as senatorial courtesy and social fraternization across party lines—have contributed dramatically to less trust and more animosity in Congress, thus increasing polarization.

> *It's hard to exaggerate how much House Republicans and Democrats dislike each other these days.*
>
> —Juliet Eilperin, *Fight Club Politics* (2006)

9. New rules for political parties. Many reforms in how we nominate, elect, and guide our political leaders—shifting the power of nomination from delegates to primaries, dismantling political machines, replacing closed-door politics with televised politics, and shrinking the influence of career politicians—aimed to democratize the system. But these changes also replaced the "middle men" who helped keep the system together with a political free-for-all in which the loudest and most extreme voices are heard above all others.

> *As these intermediaries' influence fades, politicians, activists, and voters all become more individualistic and unaccountable. The system atomizes. Chaos becomes the new normal both in campaigns and in the government itself.*
>
> —Jonathan Rauch, "How American Politics Went Insane," 2016

10. New political donors. In earlier eras, money in American politics tended to focus on candidates and parties, while money from today's super-rich donors tends to focus on ideas and ideology—a shift that also tends to advance polarization.

11. New political districts. Widespread gerrymandering—defined as manipulating district boundaries for political advantage—contributes significantly to polarization, most obviously by making candidates in gerrymandered districts worry more about being "primaried" by a more extreme member of their own party than about losing the general election.

12. The spread of media ghettos. The main features of the old analog media—including editing, fact-checking, professionalization, and the privileging of institutions over individuals—served as a credentialing system for American political expression. The distinguishing feature of the new digital media—the fact that anyone can publish anything that gains views and clicks—is replacing that old system with a non-system that is atomized and largely leaderless. One result made possible by this change is that Americans can now live in media ghettos. If I wish, I can live all day every day encountering in my media travels only those views with which I already agree. Living in a media ghetto means less that my views are shaped and improved, much less challenged, than that they are hardened and made more extreme; what might have been analysis weakens into partisan talking points dispensed by identity-group leaders; moreover, because I'm exposed only to the most cartoonish, exaggerated versions of my opponents' views, I come to believe that those views are so unhinged and irrational as to be dangerous. More broadly, the new media resemble and reinforce the new politics, such that the most reliable way to succeed in either domain is to be the most noisome, outrageous, and polarizing.

13. The decline of journalistic responsibility. The dismantling of the old media has been accompanied by, and has probably helped cause, a decline in journalistic standards. These losses to society include journalists who will accept poor quality in pursuit of volume and repetition, as well as the blurring and even erasure of boundaries between news and opinion, facts and non-facts, and journalism and entertainment. These losses feed polarization.

What have we learned so far from this survey of polarization causes? I'd say, four things. I'd also say, not enough to get to the heart of the matter.

For starters, we could probably make the list longer. For example, we could plausibly argue that rising income inequality should be added (though in my view the evidence on this one is ambiguous). Second, we can see that some of these causes are ones we either can't do much about or wouldn't want to even if we could. Third, few if any of these causes contain the quality of intentionality: None of them wake up each morning and say, "Let's polarize!" Even those coming closest to reflecting the intention to polarize, such as gerrymandering, reflect other and more fundamental intentions, such as winning elections, advancing a political agenda, or gaining clicks or viewers.

The fourth conclusion is the most important. None of these 13 causes *directly* perpetuate polarization. They are likely what analysts would call distal (ultimate) causes, but they are not proximal (immediate, direct) causes. They seem to have shaped an environment that incentivizes polarization, but they are not themselves the human words and deeds that polarize.

And so our baker's-dozen list ultimately doesn't satisfy. We need a 14th cause, arguably the most important one. It's certainly the most direct and immediate, the most proximal, cause of polarization.

14. The growing influence of certain ways of thinking about each other. These polarizing habits of mind and heart include:

- Favoring binary (either/or) thinking.
- Absolutizing one's preferred values.
- Viewing uncertainty as a mark of weakness or sin.

- Indulging in motivated reasoning (always and only looking for evidence that supports your side).
- Relying on deductive logic (believing that general premises justify specific conclusions).
- Assuming that one's opponents are motivated by bad faith.
- Permitting the desire for approval from an in-group ("my side") to guide one's thinking.
- Succumbing intellectually and spiritually to the desire to dominate others (what Saint Augustine called *libido dominandi*).
- Declining for oppositional reasons to agree on basic facts and on the meaning of evidence.

These ways of thinking constitute the actual precipitation of polarization—the direct and immediate causes of holding exaggerated and stereotyped views of each other, treating our political opponents as enemies, exhibiting growing rancor and aggression in public life, and acting as if common ground does not exist.

What's the lesson here? Although we didn't think our way into polarization—larger and more distal forces shaped the prospects for it—we'll need largely to think our way out. At this point in the process, unless some cataclysmic social change (economic collapse, another world war) does it for us, the first thing to change to get out of this mess is our minds.

One final consideration. It would be nice to make a straightforward "us versus them" enemies list when it comes to who's to blame for polarization. But the fact is, none of us is pure—besides which the impulse to create an enemies list is part of the problem, not part of the solution. Some of us are more inclined to polarizing habits than others; some of us when we foster polarization are more aware of what we're doing than others; and some of us (more and more of us, it seems) make a pretty good living these days out of encouraging and participating in polarization. But the habits and temptations of polarization are always with all of us. That includes you and me, by the way. The fault, dear reader, is not just in our 13 stars, but also in ourselves.

GETTING RIGHT WITH LINCOLN

In the late 1930s, President Franklin Roosevelt, outraged over U.S. Supreme Court decisions hostile to the New Deal, proposed expanding the number of Supreme Court justices. His so-called "court-packing" scheme failed, and few of FDR's admirers today view this episode as an admirable moment in his presidency.

Here's a footnote to this history: Both FDR and his Attorney General, Homer Cummings, tried to recruit Abraham Lincoln to their cause. After all, Roosevelt pointed out, the Great Emancipator himself had favored expanding the number of Supreme Court justices. After all, Cummings added, after the infamous *Dred Scott* case of 1857, in which the Court held that African Americans cannot be citizens and that Congress had no power to exclude slavery from the territories, Lincoln too had strongly criticized the Supreme Court. Lincoln and FDR were of like mind on this point!

The great Lincoln scholar David Herbert Donald, under whom I studied, years ago wrote a wonderful essay called "Getting Right with Lincoln." Donald shows that, beginning shortly after Lincoln's death in 1865 and continuing through the present, one of the most predictable and frequently recurring strategies in U.S. partisan politics is the attempt to recruit Lincoln.

For example, during the political battles over Reconstruction in the late 1860s and 1870s, both Radical Republicans in Congress and their most hated enemies claimed Lincoln as their hero and guide. The result was what Donald calls "a ghoulish tugging at Lincoln's shroud." And that was only the beginning.

In countless political utterances over the decades, Lincoln's words and deeds have been cited strongly to defend—and staunchly to oppose—the Greenback movement, Prohibition, the League of Nations, the New Deal, the World Court, states' rights, socialism, communism, the Republican Party platform of the day, the Democratic Party platform of the day, and sundry other philosophies and causes.

For example, in the mid-1990s, shortly after Donald published his biography, *Lincoln*, I had lunch with him in (yes, this is true) Lincoln, Massachusetts. He'd just completed a national book tour, and so I asked him, what question had he heard most often? Answer: "Was Lincoln gay?" It seems that many writers at the time were speculating about Lincoln's friendship with a young law partner, Joshua Speed, although most historians (including Donald) agree that little or no evidence suggests that Lincoln was gay or that he ever had homosexual experiences. Nonetheless, Lincoln in the 1990s was being recruited to yet another cause.

Today, what should we make of this phenomenon? In particular, since Lincoln lived during the most polarized and rancorous era in U.S. history, what lessons might we living in a similarly polarized and rancorous era learn from him? Is it authentically possible for "us, the living" to get right with Lincoln?

My first reaction to the question is "Be careful!" We know from our history how vacuous and dishonest—and tempting!—it can be to suggest that one's cause has been blessed by Lincoln.

But my second reaction is "Let's try!" Lincoln is one of our greatest leaders. His days of trial are reminiscent of ours. And God knows we could use the help. So in that spirit, and with our current crisis of polarization in mind, let's look first to Lincoln's political philosophy, and then to questions of his temperament and epistemology.

Lincoln's political philosophy consisted of only a few ideas, all deeply held, and he believed that America itself was based on these ideas. He said in 1861 that he "never had a feeling politically that did not spring from the sentiments embodied in the Declaration of Independence." In the same speech, he said that the "great principle or idea" in the Declaration was giving "liberty" to Americans and "hope to the world" that in due time "*all* should have an equal chance." At Gettysburg in 1863, he says the same thing: America was "conceived in liberty" and "dedicated to the proposition that all men are created equal." Lincoln spoke of democracy like Tocqueville did, and like Walt Whitman did, as both the nation's form of government and its special reason for existing. He believed that U.S. democracy was "the last best hope of earth."

He was a largely self-made man who believed in hard work and just rewards for hard work. He viewed honesty as a primary democratic virtue. Throughout his life, he distrusted political passion and was deeply committed to the use of reason. Arguably his highest political commitment was to the rule of law, which more than any other factor explains his fierce determination to preserve the Union.

Although not a conventionally religious man, he spoke of transcendence more intensely and more beautifully than any other American president, in part because he had experienced great personal suffering, and in part because he believed (with Shakespeare's Hamlet) that "a divinity shapes our ends, rough hew them how we will."

What can we glean from this philosophy? The topic of "American identity" is popular today among some public intellectuals who worry that in recent decades America has lost its identity. They suggest that we're so divided, mistrustful, and angry with one another that we no longer have a shared moral understanding of who we are. What's needed, in this telling, is a new story—a fresher and more unifying conception of what America is.

We do seem to have lost our shared story. But I don't think we'll fix what's broken by telling ourselves a new one. People almost never discover new ideas about who they are; instead, they refresh old ones and proceed from there. What refreshes is being the same, only more so, and on purpose. And for my money, what we need today for this identity-shaping progress is exactly what Lincoln left us. Our truest vision of the future is the good old stuff about liberty, equality, rule of law, hard work, honesty, transcendence, and best hope, only more so, and on purpose. We won't find another story. Either we'll deepen and continue to expand the one we have—the one Lincoln told better than anyone—or we won't have one.

What of Lincoln's general habits of mind and intellectual temperament? His epistemic approach to political questions? We've seen the relevance for today of *what* he thinks. Now let's examine the crucial relevance of *how* he thinks.

In a speech in the U.S. House of Representatives in 1848, he said:

> *The true rule, in determining to embrace, or reject any thing, is not whether it have* any *evil in it; but whether it have more of evil, than of good. There are few things* wholly *evil, or* wholly *good. Almost every thing, especially of governmental policy, is an inseparable compound of the two; so that our best judgment of the preponderance between them is continually demanded.*

Many of Lincoln's political contemporaries, especially in the 1850s, believed the exact opposite. They argued that, in fact, most things *are* either wholly good or wholly evil, and that politics consists of either/or choices between right and wrong, virtue and sin.

In arguing differently, Lincoln reveals a way of thinking that he never abandoned, even in his darkest moments. The idea is that I can find something of value even in views I oppose, just as my opponents, at least on their better days, can find something of value in my views. Lincoln believed that our shared history as

Americans—what he called the "mystic chords of memory"—did not necessarily foster this form of civic friendship, but did make it possible.

A related way of thinking, which Lincoln also exemplifies, is the idea that many great struggles are less contests of good versus bad than of good versus good. The maxim pertains both to ideas and people. Let's start with ideas.

Saving the Union is good. Freeing the slaves is good. As the nation lurched toward civil war, these two goods conflicted with each other. Lincoln's highest commitment was to the former, but he ultimately struggled for the latter as well, and in the end sacrificed his life for both. He was self-consciously struggling, painfully and imperfectly, with what liberal philosophers a century later would call "goods in conflict."

Preserving the rule of law is good. Winning the war is good. In 1861, the two conflicted. Lincoln arguably weakened the rule of law that year when he unilaterally suspended the writ of *habeas corpus*, essentially on grounds of military necessity. But he never viewed the choice in easy-to-decide terms of good versus bad.

Most importantly, Lincoln never saw his opponents as his enemies. Even in war, the harshest of human social struggles, he did not demonize, did not indulge in abusive stereotypes, did not falsely exaggerate disagreements, and did not treat his opponents as either less than human or too depraved and delusional to even seek to understand.

Jefferson Davis, the president of the Confederate States of America, was Lincoln's opposite in many ways, including temperament. In 1861 he said: "Our people now look with contemptuous astonishment on those with whom they had been so recently associated." Lincoln did not think or talk that way. Nor did he respond in kind to personal attacks, even as they rained down on him without cessation. Remarkably, when

Lincoln in his Second Inaugural said "malice toward none," he meant it.

Let's sum up. Few aspirations are either wholly good or wholly bad. Few struggles are between good people and bad people. These twin intellectual approaches defined Lincoln, just as they define today the difference between a mentality based on ideology and one based on doubt and humility.

The main American story in the middle and late 1850s is the nation's movement toward violence and civil war. During these years things fell apart; the center could no longer hold; force replaced argument; defiance replaced accommodation. What Lincoln called the better angels of our nature seemed to desert us. Trying with great courage to preserve a Union that was tearing itself apart, Lincoln again and again reveals a mentality that rejects dogmatism, embraces pragmatism, and seeks compromise.

On the surface, these qualities can seem less than heroic, and they help to explain why many of Lincoln's contemporaries viewed him as dithering and indecisive. Faced with constant conflict, he was always seeking to soften the edges, reassure and often placate opponents, carve out more room to maneuver, and look for ways to keep the conversation going, no matter how badly it was going.

The ideologues around him—and there were many—never really trusted him. Many viewed him as a weakling. Lincoln's feelings toward them are revealing. He tells his secretary that these radical men are "utterly lawless" and "the unhandiest devils in the world to deal with," but "after all their faces are set Zionwards." They're doctrinal and reckless, Lincoln seems to be saying, but they're walking toward the promised land of freedom for all. Here we get perhaps our deepest look into Lincoln's approach to people and conception of politics.

Lincoln had strong convictions, and ended up giving his life for them, but he was fundamentally averse to ideology. This quality in him was seldom praised and often disparaged. In politics, Lincoln was typically noncommittal, seeming to want things both ways. He would bewilder his colleagues by frequently telling them, "My policy is to have no policy." He would change his mind, equivocate, and propose half-measures that seemed to displease everyone. Prominent men with whom he worked were usually exasperated and often furious with him.

A mentality based on ideology most commonly expresses itself in self-righteousness, angry denunciations of everyone except fellow believers, and political action in which doctrinal purity is the highest concern. Lincoln was surrounded by such people, as the mid-19th century was the angriest and most polarized era in U.S. history. But he was never one of them.

He was not a member of a political faction or caucus. He was not the advocate of a spelled-out doctrine. He had a remarkable ability to work with, and ultimately win the loyalty of, leaders of nearly diametrically opposed views. All his life Lincoln told people that Henry Clay of Kentucky, who was often called "The Great Compromiser," was his "beau ideal of a statesman."

Stylistically, Lincoln chose humor over vitriol, understanding over judgment, telling stories over delivering lectures, and making suggestions over giving orders. A strong and confident man, but one who also experienced dark depression, he was mild-mannered. His capacity for empathy was striking to the people around him.

Lincoln was a poet-president and the greatest American of his generation. Our least-educated president, he may have been our wisest and most eloquent. He likely saved the country that he died for. We continue to live in his shadow, even if we're less aware of that fact than we used to be, and his words continue to haunt and inspire us.

In this light, asking ourselves today "What would Lincoln do?" is understandable and proper. But we should also appreciate why the world has little noted and not long remembered those countless attempts since 1865 to use Lincoln in the service of fixed dogmas and partisan quarrels. Lincoln's legacy—everything he stood for—is unsuited to these narrow purposes, which helps to explain why we care about him in the first place. We'll always be trying to get right with Lincoln, but our efforts will disappoint unless we also try to get Lincoln right.

IN DEFENSE OF THE PRACTICAL POLITICIAN

Is any group in America today more reviled and detested than professional politicians? In 2016, I spent a week driving through Louisiana, Mississippi, Tennessee, Kentucky, and southern Ohio interviewing blue-collar Americans about politics. I learned a lot, but by far the loudest and most consistent message from these interviews was contempt for professional politicians. National opinion polls confirm that most Americans simply no longer believe that elected officials, including those from their own party, are honest or can be trusted even to try to do what's right for the country.

These beliefs have profound consequences. To take only one obvious example, one of the most dynamic forces in U.S. politics in decades has been the Trump movement, and much of former President Trump's appeal derives from the fact that he's "not a politician." Amazingly, a Pew survey finds that a majority of the American public now believes that "ordinary Americans" could do a better job of solving the country's problems than elected officials.

This isn't right. Whatever the problems in our politics—and yes, there are many!—something is deeply wrong in any society in which the governed hold the governing in this much contempt. I'm not sure of everything we'll need to do as a society to fix this problem, but I do have one idea. It involves remembering something distinctly undramatic that happened in a little college town in Kentucky. In 1962. Involving a 39-year-old guy from Mississippi. Who wanted to be governor one day. And who taught me Sunday school.

In April of 1962, William F. Winter of Grenada, Mississippi, was serving as state tax collector, a post to which he'd been elected in 1959. Previously he had served three terms as a state legislator. He was visiting Centre College in Danville, Kentucky, that month, as he told the assembled students, "as a practicing politician seeking to discuss compromise in politics." He titled his remarks "In Defense of the Practical Politician." Today, when Americans seem unified about nothing except that we all disdain the "practical politician," both his argument in the speech and his subsequent political experience in Mississippi seem startlingly relevant.

He told the students that he did not come to Kentucky "espousing compromise" as a "cynical, smoke-filled-room, money-under-the-table concept," but rather "as that process that has reason as its chief constituent and that permits order and progress to be substituted for impasse and frustration."

Ever the politician, he flattered the students by reminding them that Kentucky, perhaps largely by virtue of its geography, "has provided so many of America's tempering and conciliating voices," including Henry Clay ("whose name has become synonymous with the fine art of compromise"), Kentucky's "native son" Abraham Lincoln, former U.S. Chief Justice Fred Vinson, and former U.S. Vice President (and Centre College alumnus) Alben Barkley. These leaders

> *were not grim, narrow-minded fanatics insistent on every letter of their position as if it were providentially inspired. These rather were reasonable men, conscious that they did not have all the answers and willing to concede to others the possibility that they, too, might be at least partially right.*

Winter then carefully interrogates the concept of compromise. Is all compromise beneficial? No. The readiness to compromise is essential to serving the public interest, Winter argues, but whether any particular compromise is worthy or unworthy depends on the "sincerity, intelligence, and honesty" of the individuals involved, exercising judgments "for which no manual can be written." There is no formula for compromise that can guarantee its success.

Is compromise typically an easier course of action than its opposite? No. Compromise on important issues involves "more real anguish" for the politician than "any other area of political experience." For "what legislator worth his salt has not lain awake at night and wrestled with his conscience as he pondered the eternal problem of expedience versus judgement?"

Winter knew from experience whereof he spoke. In 1962, he was a moderate in a state in which the word "moderate" had been transformed into a term of abuse. For example, the governor of Mississippi in 1962 was Ross Barnett, an extreme racial segregationist. His campaign song (I remember hearing it often as a child), "Roll with Ross," included this verse:

He's for segregation 100 percent
He's not a moderate, like some other gent
He'll fight integration with forceful intent

His campaign brochure (*Dynamic Leadership—To Keep Segregation and Improve Our Standard of Living*) boasted: "Ross Barnett is OPPOSED to 'moderation' in any form."

These were winning slogans in Mississippi in 1962. So William Winter, the moderate reformer who wanted to be governor one day, knew very well the stress and anguish experienced by the politician who must constantly calibrate when, and in what ways, to speak out even for "moderation," much less the progressive change that the reformer in him seeks.

Is standing up for "judgement" over "expedience" worth losing the next election? For Winter, the question is hard, not easy, to answer. But he argues that political expediency "should not automatically be made a matter of reproach" and insists that "It is not merely cynical to say that a defeated politician can't help anybody."

Is "any politician who ever concedes anything lacking in courage?" Winter argues that often "the very opposite is true." In many cases, "perhaps most," the

> *willingness to compromise involves great courage . . . Some of the most courageous public officials I have known have been the quietly dedicated men of reason who have worked under the most unrelenting pressures to gain acceptance of unpopular but necessary agreements, while bombastic orators denounced them as traitors or worse.*

Are logrolling and political favor-trading—the stuff of which many political compromises are actually made—bad for our democracy? No:

> *A dam in Wyoming or an air base in Texas is usually worth more to a President in the enactment of his program than the hoopla that attends the adoption of his party's platform . . . Let me mention that I emphasize this without apology. It is simply one of the most effective working tools that a political leader has . . .*

Finally, does American politics suffer from too many career politicians? Would our government be purer if it were more frequently led by political outsiders? No. Our history shows that success in politics is quite different from, and usually "more difficult" than, for example, success in business or the military.

That's why "the most effective political executives and legislators have been by and large the men who have come out of politically oriented backgrounds." Therefore, when all is said and done, we Americans

> *owe much to the practical politician and the adjustments he brings to the inexact science of government. If he is less than certain, it is because he knows, with [Oliver Wendell] Holmes, that certitude is not always the test of certainty. If he is less than an intellectual, it is because he knows that not all answers are found in books. If he is less than perfect, it is because he is dealing with less than perfect men.*

About five months after he delivered these remarks, some less than perfect men—men of unwavering commitment to principle who believed that compromise is treason and that moderation is cowardice—decided that the U.S. Supreme Court had no authority to require the University of Mississippi to enroll James Meredith, a young African American. One of those men was Governor Barnett. In a series of emotional public appeals—"We must either submit to the unlawful dictates of the Federal government or stand up like men and tell them, never!"—the governor urged white Mississippians to gather at the University in force to prevent Meredith's enrollment. Mississippians responded, and on the night of September 30, 1962, two people were killed and several hundred were injured in what amounted to a state-sponsored riot on and around the University campus in Oxford, Mississippi.

William Winter, privately appalled by the governor's behavior, was among the small number of Mississippi officials who publicly criticized Barnett. Yet his criticisms were mildly stated and almost always indirect. For example, in a March 1963 speech in Vicksburg, Mississippi, he observed, without mentioning the governor by name or the Ole Miss riot specifically, that "very few mobs ever spontaneously and automatically form." But "regardless of what motivates unthinking men to take the law into their own hands, it is the clear and unmistakable duty of Southern politicians to see that it does not happen." He then called for new political leadership that would

> *appeal to the best that is in us—not the worst; to our higher selves not our baser instincts. Only in this way can our section [of the country] diminish some of the tensions that have already caused us so much grief and even now threaten more . . . [Mississippi needs a leader who] can successfully turn his people from a preoccupation with the race issue and the supercharged emotions of anxiety, fear, and hate . . .*

For new state priorities, Winter favored improved public education and economic development. For the "ever-present problems of race relations," he urged a search for solutions "other than the bull-whip and the shotgun." The speech's overarching theme was that "the South will be able to prosper and progress only as it increasingly finds common cause with the nation of which it is and always has been a vital and irreplaceable part."

This way of talking, as uncontroversial as it may seem today, was not particularly popular in Mississippi in 1963. Winter had to work as a "practical politician" in Mississippi for 17 more years, almost certainly experiencing more disappointments than joys and even on good days usually having to settle for a glass half full, before finally achieving, in 1979, his goal of being elected governor of the state.

What can we learn today from William Winter's words and actions in "defense of the practical politician"? First, we can recognize that this practical politician did what he could, as often he thought he could, to improve the lives of Mississippians.

He was consistently decent, honest, empathetic, and intelligent during years in which those qualities were not widely noticeable in Mississippi politics. He worked hard with countless fellow citizens over many years, and often under extremely trying circumstances, to begin to replace "impasse and frustration" with "order and progress."

On the race issue—the first and in some ways the only issue of Mississippi politics—William Winter as a practical politician made a limited but real difference. The historian Charles C. Bolton, assessing Winter's early career, finds that after the 1959 state elections "Winter stood as one of the most-recognizable statewide officials who represented the racially moderate position in Mississippi politics." Assessing Winter's role in the state in the late 1960s, after his first (and unsuccessful) campaign for governor, the historian Joseph Crespino describes Winter in 1967 as "a moderate reformer who represented the earliest incarnation of the New South Democratic leadership" that in the 1970s would include governors such as Jimmy Carter of Georgia and Reubin Askew of Florida.

Serving in the state's most important office from 1980 to 1984, Winter was certainly one of the best Mississippi governors of the 20th century—in part because he had worked hard for, and won, the support and respect of the great majority of the state's black leaders. After leaving office and the pursuit of office in the early 1990s, he embraced racial healing and racial justice as central personal priorities. He led the William Winter Institute for Racial Reconciliation at the University of Mississippi and became the nearly universally acknowledged senior leader of Mississippi progressivism.

The great Mississippi writer William Faulkner once suggested that the artist's goal is to put "a scratch on the face of anonymity." Faulkner surely made his scratch. In the realm of Deep South politics in the second half of the 20th century, so did William

Winter, and I don't know of many others who can make a better or more honorable claim.

What traits most define this man and this career? I can think of three—all three of which seem to be in short supply and held in low regard today.

First, William Winter was a grown-up. He had an adult character structure, reflective of qualities such as the capacity to cooperate with others, the recognition of one's own limitations, the willingness to see issues from different sides, reasonableness, and the strength of character to hold in check the natural human tendencies toward narcissism and selfishness. How are these qualities faring in our public life today?

Second, William Winter was a depolarizer. His whole approach to politics was based on the idea that, despite our deeply felt and often painful differences, we can find ways to live together and make progress together. Arguably today's most significant political trend is polarization. Regarding the race issue, Ross Barnett's days are over. But regarding the values of compromise and political realism, the Ross Barnetts of this world—"He's no moderate, like some other gent"—are growing in number and riding high and sassy.

Finally, and perhaps most significantly, William Winter was a professional politician, a lifelong political insider. That meant that if he wanted to keep his job, or gain a better one, he had to focus not solely—and often not even mainly—on the merits of issues, but also on the realities of power and the chances of winning the next election. For the professional politician, issues matter, but so do interests, which means that much of the stuff and glue of everyday politics is transactional, consisting of bargaining, trading, and dealmaking. Unlike the activist or the amateur politician, who is often fueled by passion, a professional politician such as Winter is required by his circumstances to maintain a measure of detachment. Today's front-page crisis is important, but so are the institutions and the interlocking relationships that will remain in place after today's front-page crisis is over.

It turns out that *wisdom* is not a cornpone notion or a synonym for "intelligent" or "good." In recent years, a substantial academic literature finds that wisdom is its own thing: a distinctive quality of mind and heart, rare and invaluable, and not like anything else. In this literature, several traits appear again and again in definitions of wisdom. Pro-social attitudes and behaviors that reflect compassion and concern for the common good. Pragmatic knowledge of life and the use of that knowledge to make socially constructive decisions. An ability to cope with ambiguity and uncertainty, and to see multiple points of view. Emotional stability and mastery of one's own feelings. A capacity for reflection and self-understanding.

The list reads like a description of William Winter. More importantly, it reads like a description of his Practical Politician. What are a republic's prospects, one is forced to wonder, if its voters and politicians turn away from wisdom?

BLUE SAID, RED SAID

Once upon a time, liberals and conservatives used many of the same words and phrases to convey the same or similar meanings. Today, not so much. Like other aspects of our lives—where we live, who we befriend, and even what we eat and how we dress—how Americans speak increasingly reflects their political identities. Though we seldom fully realize it, not just our ideas, but the very words and phrases we use to express them typically come out of our mouths already distinctly colorized as red or blue, signaling to others our partisan political affiliation as clearly as if we were wearing ID badges.

The trend is almost entirely harmful. Shall we count the ways? It reinforces stereotypes. It fosters group-think. It makes accurate disagreement, the lifeblood of democratic discourse, harder to achieve. It contributes to mutual incomprehension. It permits us (wittingly or unwittingly) to use language for the dubious purposes of virtue-signaling and in-group bonding. It replaces authentic personal expression with stylized and formulaic expression. It instantly communicates to others a colorized persona in ways that we ourselves may not fully recognize, or recognize at all. Most of all, it wars against a shared language, thus making cross-party communication, the great imperative of our era, all but impossible.

So let's reflect on this corrosive trend and ask ourselves what, if anything, we should try to do about it. How does language colorization work? Let's examine the phenomenon at three levels.

The first and probably simplest level is *rhetorical framing*—which for our purposes can be defined as selecting and constantly repeating words and phrases that make your side look good and the other side look bad. Sometimes the technique is perfectly valid. After all, there's nothing wrong with saying what you want to say, how you want to say it. I'd put the Left's use of "common sense gun safety" in this category.

But often enough the technique is little more than describing your opponents' views with loaded words that your opponents themselves would never dream of using. Thus "pro-life" becomes "anti-choice," climate change skeptics become "deniers," favoring gun control becomes "opposing the Second Amendment," and favoring immigration becomes support for "open borders." In short, blues consciously select blue words and concepts to name red positions, and vice versa. A main result of this truly bipartisan technique is the escalating mutual mistrust and resentment.

A second level of language colorization is *rhetorical appropriation*—which for our purposes can be defined as force-changing the meaning of your opponents' words in order to attack your opponents. One highly visible current example is "fake news," which was originally coined by liberals to mean "statements that are untrue," but has already been almost entirely appropriated by conservatives to mean "statements that liberals like."

Consider also "politically correct." That infamous term emerged several decades ago on the political Left. I remember it well and used it often. Largely tongue-in-cheek, and in part a comic echo of the old Communist "party line," "politically correct" essentially meant "consistent with our political philosophy." But today the term is used almost exclusively by conservatives to mean in effect "crazy stuff liberals say."

A third example is "family values." The term emerged on the pro-family Right in the late 1970s to mean "supportive of the traditional family." But within a decade the term had been largely (though not completely) appropriated by liberals as an epithet denoting basically "narrow-mindedness about sexuality."

The third way in which we colorize our words today is the most subtle, interesting, and important way. Let's call it *rhetorical intuition*. It's less about political spinning or even specific words and phrases than about ethically based styles of expression and, ultimately, ways of understanding the world.

As developed by the psychologist Jonathan Haidt and others, moral foundations theory suggests that liberals are strongly committed to the foundational values of *fairness* (reciprocity, justice, giving others their due) and *care* (doing the opposite of harm). For conservatives, the spectrum of desirable values is somewhat wider. While they do embrace the values of fairness and care, conservatives also tend to place important emphases on the values of *loyalty* (commitment to my group, patriotism), *authority* (respect for proper rules and guidance), and *sacredness* (sanctity, purity). Moral foundations theory also suggests that both conservatives and liberals are strongly, albeit in somewhat differing ways, committed to the value of *liberty* (freedom, the opposite of oppression).

It seems plausible that, in this era of polarization, the political colorization of our language stems in part from these differences in moral foundations. Let's try out several examples.

On *fairness* and *care*: Probably the most salient and ideologically coherent term on the political Left today is "social justice," which unites in nearly perfect form these two values.

On *loyalty*: While the term "American exceptionalism" was coined by (I suspect mainly liberal) scholars seeking to understand what might be distinctive in U.S. history, today the term is used largely by conservatives as a litmus-test phrase to affirm their patriotism while implying that liberal opponents do not sufficiently love their country.

On *sacredness*: Conservatives are far more likely than liberals to speak of the "sanctity of human life" and the "sanctity of marriage" and to view the body metaphorically as a temple.

More broadly, the conservative values template tends to produce a style of expression that the great sociologist David Riesman called "inner-directed." *I am what I am—let others think what they will.* In contrast, the liberal values template tends to produce a style of expression that is more what Riesman called "other-directed." *I am what I am—in sensitivity to others.*

This difference may help to explain why liberals frequently endorse "dialogue," stress the importance of "diversity" and "inclusiveness," and emphasize the importance of a "safe space" in which group members do not feel attacked or distressed. Their style often tends toward the invitational. Many of their sentences end with question marks. They see the value of sitting in a circle. *I am what I am—in sensitivity to others.*

Conservatives, by contrast, often mistrust such relationship-centered words and usually prefer alternative language. When it comes to speech, they tend to favor clear, formal, and comparatively fewer rules. They desire to speak their minds as freely as possible and are often wary of being coached on how to be more sensitive. They don't particularly value sitting in a circle. To use an old religious term, they instead tend to respect the concept of "witness." They explain themselves. Their style often tends toward the declarative. They often de-emphasize the emotional and the psychological aspects of conversation in favor of attempts at more formal rationalism. *I am what I am—let others think what they will.*

Finally, there's the language-colorizing influence of each side's basic attitude toward the other. I want to tread here as softly as I can, because I know I'm offering overly broad generalizations, but I do believe that the great conservative sin in our public discourse today is anger, while the great liberal sin is condescension. I'm not sure which I think is worse, but I do see and dislike both, and each sin is reflected in its side's style of expression. For conservatives, the sin is evidenced mainly in the harshness in the voice, the insistence, the heat. For liberals, it's in the dulcet tone, the style that seeks graciously to educate those in need of it.

These less overt but more primary forms of colorization reveal themselves in tone, style, and body language as much as or more than they do in specific words or phrases. In this sense, speaking red or blue is more dialect than lexicon. At the same time, the political messaging is clear enough. If you're paying attention at all, the vibes can't be missed.

A few wrinkles. The first is that, in my experience, reds tend to favor economics and religion as explanatory models of human conduct, whereas blues, particularly in recent decades, have become significantly friendlier than reds to explanatory models rooted in psychology and the other social sciences. Why this is so, and whether and how it's connected to moral foundations, I'm not sure.

A second and likely related consideration is that, at least in my experience, blues speak bluer than reds speak red. By this I mean that blue vocabulary strikes me as more specialized, with a longer list of technical terms. Again, why this is so, I'm not sure.

A third addendum to the argument is that, as many have pointed out, both the partisan media complex and social media permit political partisans to mainline intensely colorized words and phrases 24 hours a day, all of which is largely unmediated by the old journalistic standards such as editing, fact-checking, and striving (at least in theory) for some form of balance. Surely feeding on this meat all day every day deepens our problem.

To me, the final wrinkle is the most surprising. All evidence notwithstanding, neither blues nor reds seem truly prepared to believe that they speak in dialect. In my experience, blues tend to understand their partisan dialect as mainly an expression of expertise, while conservatives tend to understand theirs as mainly a form of plain speaking.

What, then, if anything, is to be done? Here's a proposition. To get out of the mess we're in, we don't need to agree about politics and we don't need a shared morality. But we do need a shared moral language. For this shared language constitutes our only pathway toward recognizing each other's humanity and seeing what unites as well as what divides us. Today we see each other through a glass, darkly. Our aim must be to find those words that allow us to see each other face to face, in the light.

MY DEBATE WITH "DIALOGUE"

My job as president of Braver Angels involves inviting red and blue Americans in our deeply polarized nation to talk to each other. I love the work, and believe with all my heart that it's essential for the nation. But today the word most often publicly used by its advocates to describe it is "dialogue"—and for me that's a problem, a hindrance that makes the work harder. The main reason this is so is not trivial.

The essence of the problem is that "dialogue" is an almost entirely "blue" linguistic marker and institution. That's why it's no accident that liberals are typically eager for "dialogue," while many conservatives wince at the use of the term and are wary of the concept. The result, if I may be allowed a sports metaphor, is that an effort to bring together tennis players and weightlifters is being led by tennis coaches working on tennis courts. Is it any wonder that the weightlifters are often less than receptive?

Why is "dialogue" blue? And what should or can be done about it?

When it comes to modes of conversation in which people disagree, conservatives wary of "dialogue" tend to favor "debate." Unlike dialogue, debate implies a clear-cut contest—you make your best case, I'll make mine—in which, in principle, one side wins. The social benefit of debate, say its advocates, is that a vigorous contest of ideas is the best and perhaps only way for society to find the truth.

Here we encounter an irony. This conservative-favored conclusion about the way of disagreeing most conducive to the public good emerged historically as a core tenet of liberalism. The pedigree of the idea is both impressive and classically liberal. John Milton, in *Areopagitica*, his 1644 defense of free speech, asks: "Let Truth and Falsehood grapple; who ever knew Truth put to the worse in a free and open encounter?" John Stuart Mill, in *On Liberty* in 1869, argues that truth is more clearly understood by virtue of its "collision with error." Justice Oliver Wendell Holmes, in his famous dissent in *Abrams v. United States* in 1919, defending the right of anarchists to publish anti-government and anti-war propaganda, writes: "The ultimate good desired is better reached by free trade in ideas—that the best test of truth is the power of the thought to get itself accepted in the competition of the market." And the left-wing British political theorist Harold Laski wrote in 1919 that "in the clash of ideas we shall find the means of truth. There is no other safeguard of progress."

The fact that conservatives have become today's main champions of debate produces interesting social consequences. One is that on today's American college campuses, for example, conservatives more than liberals are the outspoken and principled defenders of free speech and open debate.

"Dialogue" differs significantly from debate. It's also historically a much newer idea. The fundamental spirit and activity of dialogue is careful listening to those with whom we disagree. In his 2017 essay on "The Power of Dialogue," Scott London defines dialogue as

> *a form of discussion aimed at fostering mutual insight and common purpose. The process involves listening with empathy, searching for common ground, exploring new ideas and perspectives, and bringing unexamined assumptions into the open.*

In *Dialogue and the Art of Thinking Together*, his respected 1999 book on the subject, William Isaacs defines dialogue as " a conversation in which people think together in relationship" and "a way of taking the energy of our differences and channeling it toward something that has never been created before." For Isaacs, dialogue is the best and perhaps only social strategy that can "lift us out of polarization."

The benefits of dialogue, then, say its advocates, are less stereotyped thinking about "the other side," the discovery of common ground and new ways of working together, and ultimately a richer and fuller understanding of the truth and the common good.

Dialogue and debate differ in numerous ways, but two differences are especially important. First, people in debates are not expected to change their views as a result of the debate. Quite the opposite: They are expected to try to change *other* people's views. But in dialogue, as Isaacs puts it, you

> *no longer take your own position as final. You relax your grip on certainty and listen to the possibilities that result simply from being in a relationship with others—possibilities that might not otherwise have occurred.*

Why is this idea central to dialogue? One reason is that dialogue favors conciliation over conflict. Another and probably more seminal reason is the underlying belief of dialogue leaders—supported now by a body of social science evidence—that diverse groups are wiser and can make better decisions than either homogeneous groups or gifted individuals.

The second key difference is that dialogue, unlike debate, usually incorporates the participants' personal experiences and feelings as well as their abstractly formulated philosophical positions. In debate, disembodied rationality and what the young Abraham Lincoln in 1838 called "cold, calculating, unimpassioned reason" are intended to reign alone. But in dialogue, therapeutic guidance, coaching, and subjective expression are not simply permitted, but are often expected and at times required of and by dialogue leaders.

Dialogue tends to cultivate and encourage expressions of caring. Says Wellesley College's current *Guide for Dialogue Facilitators*: "Dialogue involves a concern for the other person and seeks to not alienate or offend." The educator and philosopher Nel Noddings, who focuses on the ethics of care, says that "dialogue is such an essential part of caring that we could not model caring without engaging in it." So we're left with this question: Why do conservatives as a group embrace the traditionally liberal concept of debate and disavow dialogue, while liberals do exactly the opposite? I can think of two main answers, but let's start with one that, in my view, does *not* hold water. Some people (liberals all, so far as I know) suggest that conservatives are more reluctant than liberals to expose themselves to alternative viewpoints.

In my experience, I've found no evidence to support this thesis and quite a bit, including recent findings from researchers, to discredit it. Most conservatives are just as prepared as most liberals to engage those with whom they disagree, and the truly dogmatic personalities that refuse to engage are, it seems to me, evenly distributed ideologically. No, the issue dividing the two groups is not *whether* to engage, but *how* they prefer to engage.

So what *does* explain this polarization? First, the entire concept and practice of dialogue—who funds it, who studies and writes about it, who advocates for it, who designs it, who convenes it, and who leads it—is overwhelmingly blue. Why this is so and whether it must remain so are useful questions to pose, but for the moment let's simply admit that it's so, which of course helps explain why conservatives tend to be wary.

Second, and in my view more importantly, conservatives are generally reluctant to participate in a process in which it's expected or hoped that they will alter their views. Wellesley College's *Guide for Dialogue Facilitators* teaches that "the primary purpose of dialogue is for each person to learn from the other so that each can change and grow."

Why so many conservatives—properly, in my view—mistrust this idea is not hard to discover. It has to do with power. In the overwhelmingly blue-dominated world of American dialogue, liberals have it and conservatives don't. Here's how my friend R. R. "Rusty" Reno, the conservative editor of *First Things*, puts it:

> *In my years as a theology professor, as a rare conservative in higher education, I became accustomed to calls for dialogue on this or that issue. In almost every instance, it was a set-up for mandatory public capitulation. If someone regards abortion as a moral evil and same-sex marriage as an oxymoron, as I do, he cannot say so in a public forum, for it amounts to a sin against dialogue. It "shuts down conversation," I was told on many occasions . . . The movement from dialogue to censure and then denunciation is often a smooth one.*

Rusty seems to me to overstate his case, since I don't believe that U.S. dialogue leaders are typically guilty of bad faith. But I do recognize what he's describing. After all, in a typical U.S. dialogue, who gets to frame the questions? Set the tone? Do the coaching on how to be sensitive to others? Determine what defines "expert facilitation" and what is politically charged facilitation presenting itself as expertise? In Orwell's *Animal Farm*, we learn that "All animals are equal, but some animals are more equal than others." To extend this idea, conservatives considering whether to engage in liberal-sponsored dialogue might be displaying more than simply defensiveness or paranoia to suspect that "All voices in a dialogue are equal, but some voices are more equal than others."

What, then, can be done? Is there a creative new blend of dialogue and debate waiting to be born? Can we change our ideas about structuring the conversation so that red and blue Americans can gather in roughly equal numbers and with shared confidence for conversation aimed at rediscovering civic trust and common ground? Here are four suggestions.

Change the name. The word "dialogue" is so deeply blue I doubt anything can be done at this point to depolarize it. What's a better name for the activity? Maybe "workshop"?

Don't encourage people to change their views. I think we should stop saying that red-blue engagement means being open to moderating your views or changing your mind. Most conservatives, for understandable reasons, simply won't sign up for such a project. It's true that part of the beauty of this activity is that participants often *do* enlarge their thinking—if not about issues, then at least about each other. That is a kind of change in thinking, but not a flat either/or sort of change. But why is it necessary to imply upfront that participants are likely or expected to "change and grow," as opposed to simply permitting change and growth to happen or not happen freely, organically, and individually, as unforced and unrequired results of the activity rather than as a required component of it?

Keep teaching and coaching to a minimum. Here I mean that we should significantly cut down on things like correcting people who make insensitive remarks, intervening when someone in the group appears to be uncomfortable, or in other ways instructing participants on how they should speak to and act toward one another. Grassroots democracy is an often rough but essential activity, and my colleagues and I have found that, while it's important to establish basic conversational guardrails to ensure civility, it's also important to let people speak freely, doing as little policing as possible. On a practical level, there are definitely some things more counterproductive than liberals trying to teach conservatives how to speak, or vice versa, but not many.

Change who's in control. This reform is by far the most important, and without it none of the other changes are likely to make much difference. If today we put into one arena every person in America who funds, organizes, leads, studies, or advocates for structured red-blue conversation, you can be sure that more than 90 percent of them would be liberals. And here's the hard but inescapable truth: Meaningful red-blue engagement in America is flatly inconsistent with this fact. That's why this sociopolitical reality must change dramatically and at every level, from who pays, to who plans and designs, to who attends, to who evaluates and publicizes—otherwise what the nation needs most simply will not happen.

What's the next step? Hmm ... lemme think. Should a group of leaders interested in addressing this challenge—half-red, half-blue—come together for in-depth conversation rooted in empathetic listening and aimed at new and better collective thinking? Shall we debate? Shall we dialogue?

WHERE'S THE TRUST?

The main toxin ruining our politics and coarsening our society is the loss of trust. Not Donald Trump or Joe Biden, or evil liberals, or the dishonest media, or right-wing populism, or insufficient fervor for this or that candidate or cause—but rather the widespread and growing belief among Americans that many if not most of their fellow citizens lack basic honesty, integrity, and reliability.

It's also something we rarely discuss. We live in an age that favors almost exclusively the discussion of "them" problems—shortcomings that we can attribute to the bad conduct of a particular group. But mistrusting each other is almost by definition an "us" problem. It implicates all parties. As such, collapsing social trust can't easily be construed—though how tempting to try!—as simply another thing to blame on Donald Trump or Joe Biden, or evil liberals, or the dishonest media, or right-wing populism, or insufficient fervor for this or that candidate or cause.

Evidence of our loss of trust in one another is clear and abundant. In their influential 2020 book, *The Upswing*, the scholars Robert D. Putnam and Shaylin Romney Garrett conclude: "In round numbers, in the early 1960s nearly two thirds of Americans trusted other people, but two decades in the twenty-first century two thirds did not." A 2013 study similarly reports: "Trust in others and confidence in institutions, two key indicators of social capital, reached historic lows among Americans in 2012 in two nationally representative surveys that have been administered since the 1970s."

I saw this trend up close in 2017 with respect to Americans' political views. With colleagues and a rented bus, and partnering with wonderful local volunteers, I helped to organize 25 workshops that summer involving a total of about 400 voters in communities in Ohio, Tennessee, Virginia, Vermont, Maryland, New York, New Jersey, and Pennsylvania. Our purpose was to bring together "red" and "blue" Americans in roughly equal numbers to talk *with*, rather than simply *at* or *about*, each other.

We learned a lot about trust. For example, an extremely common belief today among both liberals and conservatives is that, if I know your position on an issue, I also know why you hold that position. Here's how it can happen. You say that you want stricter immigration laws. I believe that stricter immigration laws would harm people of color. Therefore I conclude that you favor stricter immigration laws at least partly because you don't care about people of color.

Or, you say that you support Obamacare. But for me, Obamacare means big government stamping out individual choice. Therefore I conclude that you support Obamacare at least partly because you are content to let big government stamp out individual choice.

See how it works? It's a three-step mental process in which I glide seamlessly from your policy preference, to my understanding of the bad result of that policy, to my assumption about your bad reason for preferring it.

When you see this phenomenon occur over and over again—particularly when the two sides are in the same room, actually talking to each other, and therefore ultimately holding each other accountable—it becomes quite clear that this formula for analyzing one's adversaries generates far more heat than light, far more error than truth.

And why is this flawed formula so popular? One answer is that it encourages demonization, and demonization is all the rage these days. But that only begs the question. The deeper reason, I believe, is that mistrustful Americans find it increasingly hard to assume that their political opponents have decent or even rational motives. After all, it's not natural or easy to assume that people you don't trust have basically good intentions; in fact, it may not even make sense to do so.

How deep does today's political mistrust run? Here's one clue. We'd ask, would you be interested in attending a workshop? They'd say, maybe, but I'm probably not who you want. We'd ask, why do you say that? They'd answer, because I base my views on logic and facts, and therefore don't know how to talk to people on the other side. Both conservatives and liberals earnestly offered us this insight—often.

Many Americans (and I'm one of them) are distressed by the rise of what appears to be post-fact political rhetoric, made possible by a political culture in which the flagrant distortion of truth for political purposes is normative and in which the question of what is a fact appears to be more a matter of party affiliation than objective reality. It's all terrible.

But what gave birth to this culture? The media? Bad politicians? The fact that Americans are no longer smart enough or curious enough to care about what is a fact? I don't think so. I think this culture arose mainly because we don't trust each other.

After all, even the smartest of us humans don't determine what is factual solely or even mainly by dint of personal investigation. I believe that Joe Biden won the last presidential election. But I didn't count the ballots and couldn't tell you with any precision how they were counted. I believe that human-caused climate change is real and dangerous. Yet I have zero expertise in the subject and couldn't conduct a legitimate experiment about our climate even if I wanted to. I believe what I believe about the 2020 election and climate change *only* because I trust what many people say about it. *We accept almost all of our facts mainly on the basis of trust.*

Increasingly, Americans don't trust anyone outside of their in-group to tell them what the facts are. As a result, what we sincerely believe to be the facts is increasingly a reflection of the group we belong to. In short, our problem is not that Americans have recently become disdainful of the facts. Nor is it that my side respects the facts and your side doesn't (as tempting as that is to believe). It's rather that, in a low-trust society such as ours, both the facts themselves and our ways of thinking about the facts begin to function less as public goods—things that promote shared thriving—and more as private assets that we use to define and defend our group and to attack the group's enemies.

It's possible, of course, that declining social trust is less the cause of our problems than the result of them. This argument has a familiar ring. Americans stopped trusting politicians when politicians, beginning particularly during Vietnam and Watergate, stopped being trustworthy. Americans lost trust in many key social institutions—from marriage to political parties to organized religion to news organizations—when those institutions stopped meeting people's needs and expectations. Americans stopped trusting people with whom they disagree politically when those people started embracing crazy, dangerous ideas. I concede that there is likely some truth to at least some of these claims.

But I'm more supportive of the opposite view. Even if objective social failures or other structural changes in society triggered and therefore can help to explain the decline of trust, that decline is now spreading at least partly independently of those failures and changes, feeding on itself and perpetuating itself. Whatever may have ignited this fire, it's now burning in large measure on its own, destroying social connections that are both fragile and precious.

What is to be done? Perhaps, in order to regain trust in one another, we need some big, sweeping structural and institutional changes. Reform our election laws. Change how Congress operates. Put an end to gerrymandering. Reduce the influence of money in politics. Reinvent political parties. Make journalism more responsible. Reduce inequality. Make society more just. I'm convinced that these and similar changes could contribute significantly to renewing social trust.

But I believe that we must also do something more basic. We need to talk to one another. We need Americans who disagree profoundly with one another—police leaders and Black Lives Matter, Trump supporters and never-Trumpers, Southern Baptists and Unitarian Universalists—in the room together, listening to one another with respect and civility, reducing stereotyped thinking about one another by achieving accurate rather than imagined disagreement, and looking when possible for common ground and ways to work together.

Talking to one another. As simplistic and quotidian as that prescription may sound, I'm convinced that, if more trust is the goal, there's no getting around this requirement and no substitute for it. I think of it as trying to strengthen American civil society, community by community. One could also think of it as trying to rebuild American citizenship from the grassroots up. Or—perhaps this is best—it's ultimately about helping us trust one another as citizens again.

A guy from one of the workshops in Ohio summed it up about as well as possible. He said, "You don't hate who you know."

TO LOVE CONFEDERATE MONUMENTS AND CIVIL RIGHTS

Possibly alone among God's creatures, we humans saturate the physical landscape with intentional displays of moral meaning. These constructed moral declarations are part of how we name ourselves. They cry out to the living and the unborn: "This is who we are, where we stand, and how we aim to be remembered." Examples of these physical prayers include monuments, museums, flags, memorial windows, murals, roadside and other historical markers, and of course the names we choose and re-choose over time for our streets and highways, schools and universities, parks, libraries, government buildings, sports teams and mascots, lakes and reservoirs, bridges, airports, and much else.

In 2017 I spent 10 days driving around the South—Mississippi, Alabama, Tennessee, Georgia, South Carolina, and Virginia—looking at these moral markers and talking to people about them. My tour was anything but scientific, but anecdotes are to scientific data what piers are to bridges: Sometimes they develop from the former into the latter. We'll focus first on the Lost Cause and then on the Beloved Community, so we'll move in time from the Civil War of the 1860s to the civil rights movement of the 1960s.

Let's start with Confederate monuments. Particularly after the August 2017 violent protest and counter-protest in Charlottesville, Virginia, ostensibly about the city's plan to remove a statue of Robert E. Lee from the recently re-christened Emancipation Park—the former name was Lee Park—many pundits across the nation weighed in on the subject of Confederate monuments. Most commentators took one stance or its opposite in a simple choice between "keep them" and "get rid of them." It took me several days of driving around to abandon this way of thinking.

Goodness knows these memorials to the Lost Cause seem to be nearly everywhere in the South. This ubiquity itself creates cultural meaning. A college professor in Johnson City, Tennessee, usefully put it to me this way:

> *The sheer number of monuments is such a forceful presence, forming a public identity that can negate other identities. So consideration of individual monuments can't be separated from the meaning of the aggregate.*

As a nearly lifelong Civil War buff, I've studied and loved Civil War monuments for decades, including those in my native South. I grew up in Mississippi, and it was and (I admit) remains curiously moving to know that in nearly every county seat in the state one can find, usually less than a block from the First Baptist Church, a county courthouse in the lawn of which is a stately Confederate statue. It is usually a lone Confederate soldier atop a tall shaft, frequently displaying a florid inscription in praise of those who served and died for the Confederate States of America.

Here's one of the tributes (the words come from Jefferson Davis) inscribed on the Monument to Women of the Confederacy in Jackson, Mississippi, honoring the women

> *Whose pious ministrations to our wounded soldiers soothed the last hours of those who died far from the objects of their tenderest love, whose domestic labors contributed much to supply the wants of our defenders in the field, whose zealous faith in our cause shone a guiding star undimmed by the darkest clouds of war, whose fortitude sustained them under all the privations to which they were subjected, whose floral tribute annually expresses their enduring love and reverence for*

> *our sacred dead; and whose patriotism will teach their children to emulate the deeds of our revolutionary sires.*

As a historian, this language fascinates me. As a Southerner, it both attracts and dismays me. As a human being, it moves me deeply. At the same time, my recent drive-around changed my thinking about these memorials. I'm now more doubtful of their worth, for three reasons.

First, as my friend from Tennessee notes, there are simply too many of them saying too many confrontational things in too many prominent places. As the centerpieces of what was, from the 1870s through the 1910s, an astonishingly comprehensive and successful South-wide campaign to memorialize the Lost Cause, Confederate monuments as a group convey an essentially state-endorsed creed: "This is who we are." But of course, that's not true.

Confederate monuments are not who "we" are. There have always been what the historian Charles Reagan Wilson of the University of Mississippi calls "many Souths," not just one, and certainly not just one Southern "we" consisting of white citizens wishing to glorify the Lost Cause. No one group or cause or memory, no matter how significant, can define the South. Here, too, in my Father's house are many rooms.

The second cause of my growing doubt about the monuments concerns one of the main defenses mounted on their behalf. These monuments, their defenders say, are primarily ways for (white) Southerners to honor their dead and remember their history and heritage. But of course, that's not quite right.

The great majority of early Confederate monuments, unveiled from the 1870s through the early 1880s, were located in cemeteries. Usually sponsored by local ladies' memorial associations, they were more about mourning the dead than perpetuating a cause. Their emotional appeal is typically more somber and private than aggressive and political. An inscription on the Monument to the Gettysburg Dead (unveiled in 1875), located in the Laurel Grove Cemetery of Savannah, Georgia, says:

On Fame's eternal camping ground,
Their silent tents are spread,
And glory guards, with silence round,
The bivouac of the Dead.

Monument to the Gettysburg Dead, Laurel Grove Cemetery, Savannah, Georgia

But by the 1890s, owing largely to the labors of new patriotic groups such as the United Daughters of the Confederacy and the Sons of Confederate Veterans, the location of new monuments had shifted largely from cemeteries to courthouses, statehouses, and public thoroughfares and parks, just as the new monuments' emotional appeal—their aesthetics and poetic inscriptions—had shifted from funerary feelings of grief to political myth-making expressed with nearly religious fervor.

Most of all, these later monuments insist on the moral rightness of the Southern cause. The message is not subtle. A Confederate monument I visited in Greenville, South Carolina, says:

> *All lost, but by the graves where martyred heroes rest, he wins the most who honor saves. Success is not the test. The world shall yet decide in truth's clear far off light, that the soldiers who wore the gray and died with Lee were in the right.*

Confederate monument, Greenville, South Carolina

You want vigilance everlasting? The same monument proclaims that the fallen soldiers of Greenville County are "resting at last in that glorious land, where the white flag of peace is never furled." Any questions about what these words mean?

If so, perhaps they can be answered by Mrs. Lizzie Pollard, the first president of the Southern Memorial Association of Fayetteville, Arkansas. In 1904, she stated:

> *These monuments we build will speak their message to unborn generations. These voiceless marbles in their majesty will stand as vindicators of the Confederate soldier. They will lift from these brave men the opprobrium of rebel, and stand them in the line of patriots. This is not alone a labor of love, it is a work of duty as well. We are correcting history.*

Statue of Robert E. Lee, Monument Avenue, Richmond, Virginia

The third cause of my change of heart concerns a difficult moral question: Can there be beauty in devotion to a flawed cause? For me, the answer is yes. I believe that slavery was morally unacceptable. I believe that Southern leaders in the 1850s were foolish, arrogant, and irrationally aggrieved. I believe that attempting to secede from the Union was a tragic mistake. I'm glad the North won that terrible war.

But do I see beauty in Robert E. Lee, who led an army whose purpose I detest? I do. Do I see nobleness in Southern women who (as one monument tells it) "loved their land because it was their own, and scorned to seek another reason why"? I do, even as I believe that loving my land because it's mine, and scorning to seek another reason why, is morally wrong and dangerous. I believe that it's possible and can be part of a good life to honor one's forbears' bravery, stamina, and commitment without favoring their political ideology.

But here's the catch: As we've seen, the most visible and important of the Confederate monuments do *not* purport to honor brave people who fought for a doubtful cause. Quite the opposite: The builders of these monuments, along with those who controlled the prominent sites on which they are located, created a style of public memorialization blending remembrance and sacralized political defiance such that the two feelings become inseparably one.

For me, that's a source of both curiosity and, increasingly, remorse. I am eager to remember with compassion and understanding those who died. But I resist with all the powers available to me being complicit in a public endorsement of the cause for which they died.

> *No nation rose so pure and fair,*
> *None fell, so pure of crime.*
>
> —Inscription on a Confederate monument in Augusta, Georgia

The white South's intense memorialization of the Lost Cause occurred more than a century ago. And no memorialization, not even this one, can become frozen in time. Memorialization happens, but so does de-memorialization.

Consider one window through which to observe these processes. The United Daughters of the Confederacy is more responsible than any other group for the Confederate monuments we see today. A century ago, the group reportedly had about 70,000 members. A perusal of the minutes of its 1917 national convention, held in Chattanooga, Tennessee, suggests a highly energetic, grassroots, volunteer-led organization dedicated to waging a comprehensive campaign to honor the Confederate dead, support Confederate veterans, vindicate Confederate history, and defend and advance the Confederate cause.

The scope of the Daughters' 1917-18 activities is breathtaking. They are completing Confederate monuments, including an unveiling in Shiloh, Tennessee—"I wish every one of you could have attended the unveiling. The day was as perfect a day as ever dawned . . . It was the greatest day in the history of the park. Conservative estimates placed the crowd at 12,000 . . . "They are raising funds for the recently deceased artist who created the Confederate monument in Arlington, Virginia, to be buried there. They are sponsoring a memorial window, to be placed in the Capitol in Washington, D.C., honoring women of the Confederacy—"the noble mothers of the sixties . . . [who] gave their gallant sons to their country." They are petitioning for highways to be renamed for Jefferson Davis, the president of the Confederacy, and supporting the creation of a school to be named for Alexander Stephens, the vice president of the Confederacy.

They are also successfully lobbying publishers and public schools to replace current history textbooks with "histories that are fair to the South." They are sending photographs of Jefferson Davis and Robert E. Lee for display in public schools. They are nurturing a national auxiliary group for young people called Children of the Confederacy. They are lobbying the U.S. Congress to refund to the Southern states the taxes on cotton collected by the federal government from 1862 to 1868, on the grounds that the taxes were collected illegally. They are passing resolutions to condemn the "hate song" called "Marching Through Georgia," urging the song's "suppression and elimination in all schools on all occasions, both public and private."

In convention plenary sessions they are singing "Dixie" (a song Abraham Lincoln loved) and "Old Black Mammy's Comin' Home." They are collecting books for a Confederate Library. They are creating a poetry and a literature of the Confederacy, including a "Catechism for Children" focusing on the war and Reconstruction. They are sponsoring children's and university-level essay contests on the Confederacy. They are awarding Southern Crosses of Honor (the award's motto is *Fortes Creantur Fortibus*: "The Brave Beget the Brave") to worthy Confederate veterans. They are lobbying for the term "Civil War" to be replaced by "War Between the States," since, as one UDC leader put it, "calling it a 'Civil War' is a complete surrender of the basic principle upon which that war was waged, the right of self-government . . ."

And much more. Through it all runs great ambition and remarkably intense devotion to the Cause. One of the convention's opening addresses, delivered by Mrs. A. A. Campbell of Wytheville, Virginia, reports that "after more than half a century of reflection, [we] are still convinced that the men who followed Lee, Jackson, Johnston, and our other immortals fought for the liberties secured to them by the Federal Constitution."

Today the United Daughters of the Confederacy has about 20,000 members. Compared to a century ago, it's not doing much, and what it does seems more quaint and anachronistic than fiery and revisionist. Their long-term decline in both membership and zeal is probably as good a marker as any for what Charles Reagan Wilson calls "the de-memorialization of the Lost Cause."

In the 12 months after the Charlottesville violence alone, about 30 Confederate monuments, mostly in the South, were removed or relocated, and many more became subjects of controversy. The day before I visited Richmond, Virginia, in part to see the massive Confederate statues along Monument Avenue, the statue of Robert E. Lee on the avenue had been spray-painted with the letters "BLM," for Black Lives Matter. In Greenville, South Carolina, I visited the Museum and Library of Confederate History, operated by the local Sons of Confederate Veterans, and during the hour or so my family and I were there, we were the only visitors. In short, with each passing year, Confederate memorialization occupies a less dominant and less secure portion of the Southern landscape.

And what's replacing it? The memorialization of the Beloved Community. Across the South, with an intensity that resembles the intensity of the United Daughters of the Confederacy in their heyday, the sons and daughters of the 1960s civil rights movement are remaking the landscape to honor their (now mostly fallen) heroes and endorse the moral rightness of their cause.

Today in Birmingham, Alabama, you can visit, as I did, the Confederate Soldiers and Sailors Monument (unveiled 1905) in a park near the Jefferson County Courthouse. But you can also visit, as I did, beautiful civil rights memorials located in the four-acre Kelly Ingram Park (repurposed in 1992) adjacent to the 16th Street Baptist Church. The church was bombed in 1963 by Ku Klux Klan members, resulting in the deaths of four African American children and the injury of many other church members. The proposal to repurpose Ingram Park came from Richard Arrington, Jr., Birmingham's first African American mayor. (Today in Birmingham you can drive down Richard Arrington, Jr. Boulevard.)

Christened "A Place of Revolution and Reconciliation," the park features a statue memorializing the four children ("Four Spirits") killed in the church bombing. It also features statues of Martin Luther King, Jr., Fred Shuttlesworth, and other local pastors who were active in the movement. Additional monuments and plaques commemorate two anonymous African American young people (the inscription says "I Ain't Afraid") and the students who, as civil rights demonstrators in 1963, were assaulted by the Birmingham police using dogs and firehoses. Across the street from the park is the Birmingham Civil Rights Institute (dedicated in 1992) whose mission is "to enlighten each generation about civil and human rights."

Four Spirits Memorial, Ingram Park, Birmingham, Alabama

"Foot soldiers of the Birmingham civil rights movement," Ingram Park, Birmingham, Alabama

This same trend is present across the South. In Richmond, on the grounds of the State Capitol, you can visit a statue of Thomas J. "Stonewall" Jackson, the famous Confederate general (unveiled in 1875 before an estimated crowd of 40,000-50,000). But on those same grounds you can also visit the Virginia Civil Rights Memorial (unveiled in 2008), featuring 18 statues of African American high school students and others who fought to desegregate Virginia's public schools in the 1950s ("It seemed like reaching for the moon"). Fittingly enough, perhaps, the memorial is located within yards of a statue of Harry F. Byrd, Sr. (unveiled in 1976), the former governor and U.S. senator who led the political and grassroots effort (under the slogan "Massive

Resistance") to prevent the desegregation of Virginia's schools in the 1950s.

Also in Richmond, you can visit a prominently located statue honoring Maggie L. Walker (unveiled in 2017), who for decades led Richmond's Independent Order of Saint Luke, a self-help society (its motto was "Succor and Employment for the Negro Woman"), and was the first African American woman to serve as president of a bank. You can visit the nearby Maggie L. Walker High School. Several blocks away from the Walker statue, the latest statue to be erected on Monument Avenue, and the first to memorialize someone other than a Confederate hero, honors Arthur Ashe, the first world-famous African American tennis player.

Statue of Maggie L. Walker, Richmond, Virginia

In Jackson, Mississippi, where I grew up, children for decades attended the Jefferson Davis Elementary School. No longer. In 2018, the name became the Barack Obama School.

When I was a child, Jackson's airport was named after Allen C. Thompson, a former Mayor whose views on racial issues were, shall we say, not advanced. Some years back, as African Americans began assuming political power (and as whites left the city), the name was changed to the Thompson–Evers Airport, curiously pairing Thompson's name with that of Medgar W. Evers, the civil rights leader murdered in 1963 by a member of the White Citizens' Council. But by 2004, the re-memorialization had been completed: Today the airport is called Jackson–Medgar W. Evers International Airport. Also, part of Highway 49 near Jackson is now called Medgar Evers Boulevard, along which you can find a library and statue memorializing Evers' life.

Civil rights museums and civil rights trails in the South are steadily multiplying. In Jackson, you can visit the new Mississippi Civil Rights Museum (opened 2017). In Ruleville, Mississippi, you can visit the Fannie Lou Hamer Museum and Memorial Garden (dedicated 2008) ("She fought racism, injustice, and poverty"). Two of the most recent and important of these new institutions, the Legacy Museum and the National Memorial for Peace and Justice, both in Montgomery, Alabama, and both dedicated in 2018, remember African Americans killed by lynching (the memorial) and victimized by enslavement and mass incarceration (the museum).

Driving north on Highway 51 near Goodman, Mississippi, I noticed that the name of that portion of the highway had been changed to Martin Luther King, Jr. Memorial Highway. The next day, as I drove into Atlanta from the south, the first three boulevards I saw were named for Martin Luther King, Jr., Joseph E. Lowery (who succeeded Dr. King as president of the Southern Christian Leadership Conference), and Ralph David Abernathy (who succeeded Lowery). The next day, near Fredericksburg, Virginia, headed toward Jefferson Davis Highway, I drove across the Martin Luther King, Jr. Memorial Bridge.

A 2015 survey published in the *New York Times* reports that, in the 11 former Confederate states, the name "Martin Luther King, Jr." is associated with 1,183 miles of roadway. The name "Jefferson Davis" is associated with 468 miles. For Robert E. Lee, the figure is 60 miles.

Fannie Lou Hamer Museum and Memorial Garden, Ruleville, Mississippi

Goodman, Mississippi

There are similarities between the memorialization of the Lost Cause and the memorialization of the Beloved Community. Both of these campaigns honor their fallen. Both glorify their heroes. Both are suffused with moral and religious fervor. And both declare that their cause is right.

There are also dissimilarities. One movement occurred more than a century ago and peaked in the 1910s. The other is occurring today and seems not to have peaked yet. A second difference concerns political influence. The ideology of the Lost Cause achieved regional hegemony, occupying the commanding heights of Southern government and society. The ideology of the Beloved Community has not (at least yet) achieved anywhere near that level of influence.

The most important difference concerns divergent understandings of race. Both movements are deeply connected to racial issues—in one case, the enslavement of African Americans, and in the other, African Americans' struggle for equal rights. At the same time, partisans of the Lost Cause addressed race primarily by ignoring it in favor of a focus on states' rights and regional loyalty, while often augmenting that approach with overt displays of racism, whereas commitment to racial equality is the very essence of what animates partisans of the Beloved Community.

I ended my tour heartened and chastened. I'm heartened that more and more of the Southern landscape now memorializes the 1960s civil rights movement. It's overdue, it's a matter of simple justice, it reflects what's best in our nation, and it makes me more hopeful about the region's future. May this effort continue, as there's much more to do.

I'm chastened because I now see that the Civil War monuments I grew up with should be removed from Southern courthouses,

Confederate monument, Fredericksburg, Virginia, cemetery

capitol grounds, and public parks and thoroughfares. I'd like to see them relocated to cemeteries, those places of remembrance and honor initially chosen as sites for them by the ladies' memorial associations of the 1870s and 1880s. Reuniting these physical tributes to the dead with the graves of the soldiers themselves and their descendants seems honorable, reverential, fitting for a multi-racial South, and properly public.

Unknown CSA soldier gravestone in Fredericksburg cemetery

On my trip, one of my most cherished experiences was visiting a cemetery in Fredericksburg, Virginia. In 1866, the Ladies Memorial Association of Fredericksburg, seeking (in their words) to "rescue from oblivion the memory of the brave," began amid the privations of the war's aftermath to raise funds for the cemetery. After much effort and sacrifice, the cemetery was dedicated in 1870. It contains the graves of Confederate veterans who died in nearby battles (many "Unknown") and others. In the middle of the cemetery, atop a grassy mound, is a 20-foot-high monument (unveiled in 1884) featuring a standing Confederate soldier. The monument's inscription is simple and moving: "To the Confederate Dead." Visiting there, I remembered.

TO RESIST AND RECONCILE

I'm not a very good Christian, but I wish I were a better one, and toward that end I study the life of A. J. Muste. I never met him—he died in 1967—and I don't ultimately share his left-wing, pacifist views, but my admiration for him continues to grow.

He was born in the Netherlands in 1885. Six years later his family immigrated to Grand Rapids, Michigan, which had a thriving Dutch community anchored in the Calvinist traditions of the Dutch Reformed Church. When young Abraham Johannes Muste first set foot on U.S. soil at Ellis Island, in New York Harbor, a hospital attendant who could speak no Dutch affectionately referred to him as "Abraham Lincoln." The Dutch-speaking child at first thought that "Abraham Lincoln" might be a town, but soon enough he began, as he put it, "to read everything by and about Lincoln that I could lay my hands on," such that his feeling for Lincoln eventually became "a part of my inmost being."

In 1909, he was ordained as a minister of the Dutch Reformed Church, but 10 years later, radicalized by his opposition to the Great War and by his involvement with striking textile workers that year in Lawrence, Massachusetts, Muste left the church and abandoned Christianity. Through the mid-1930s, he was active in labor organizing and in radical (including Trotskyite) politics. In 1936, he re-embraced his Christian faith. Over time Muste's journey led him to the Society of Friends (the Quakers) and to ministerial posts in Congregational and Presbyterian churches. But Muste's truest Christian witness, both within the church and in the larger society, expressed itself in struggles for social justice, nonviolence, and peace.

Tall, lean, and frugal, Muste had simple tastes, avoided bank accounts, and admitted to "a strong aversion to money-making."

In *Peace Agitator*, Nat Hentoff's terrific biography, Hentoff reports that Muste "gives the impression of owning only one suit."

Many people who knew him describe him as serene and, astonishingly for a political radical, almost never given to zealotry or self-congratulations. Quiet and soft-spoken, he avoided the limelight and usually did more listening than talking, even when he was in charge. He laughed often, including at himself. He was a Christian mystic who was fiercely intellectual and read constantly.

Partly owing to his study of Mohandas Gandhi, Muste in his work as a peace activist became America's foremost early-20th-century exemplar of the philosophy and tactics of nonviolent resistance. In 1949, a young student at Crozier Theological Seminary, Martin Luther King, Jr., was first exposed to these ideas when he heard Muste give a lecture on the topic. The two men became collaborators. Years later, at the height of the sit-ins and other nonviolent protests of the U.S. civil rights movement, Dr. King said: "I would say unequivocally that the current emphasis on nonviolent direct action in the race relations field is due more to A.J. than to anyone else in the country."

What I admire most about Muste is his work as a reconciler. For most of five decades he was a leader of the Fellowship of Reconciliation, a nondenominational pacifist organization committed to nonviolence and international understanding. In this work, Muste had great empathy and listened to everyone. He did not end relationships.

For example, starting in about 1955, Muste, a strong anti-communist, initiated a series of private conversations with American communists who were considering leaving the party. One of those who met with Muste during these years later said: "We had been trained to believe that there couldn't be anything decent or honest in 'liberals' who weren't in the party, but it was revealing to recognize the thread of principle that ran through everything a man such as Muste did and said. Most of the other non-Communists were thoroughly suspicious of those of us who were having doubts . . . I say this as an atheist, but if I were to be asked if I've ever known a saint, I'd have to say Muste comes close."

As a result of these and similar efforts, Muste was publicly accused of disloyalty by the Director of the FBI, J. Edgar Hoover, who in 1957 reported to a U.S. Senate investigating committee that Muste "has long fronted for Communists." Muste wrote a long letter of reply to Hoover, detailing his long-standing opposition to communism as well as his ongoing conversations with party members, and noting in closing that, while "conscientiously opposed to responding to summons to appear before any government official or agency engaged in investigating the political or religious opinions of myself or others," he [Muste] would "appreciate it" if Mr. Hoover "should have time to discuss these matters with me on a personal basis." Director Hoover did not respond.

Asked about his approach, Muste said: "One has to be both a resister and a reconciler . . . You have to be sure that when you're reconciling, you're also resisting any tendency to gloss things over; and when you're primarily resisting, you have to be careful not to hate, not to win victories over human beings. You want to change people, but you don't want to defeat them."

Part of Muste's genius in bringing people together is that he never succumbed to the belief that he spoke truth and that his opponents spoke error. He said: "You always assume there is some element of truth in the position of the other person, and you respect your opponent for hanging on to an idea as long as he believes it to be true. On the other hand, you must try very hard to see what truth actually does exist in his idea, and seize on it to make him realize what you consider to be a larger truth."

ANTHEMS

If you want to know America, study the words of our national anthems. In his terrific book *This Land That I Love*, John Shaw offers at least eight songs that qualify as true American anthems, or "songs that people sing together on ceremonial or celebratory occasions when they want to evoke, share, or express a public emotion about nationhood." The earliest is "Hail, Columbia" (1789) and the most recent is "This Land Is Your Land" (1940). In between are "The Star-Spangled Banner" (1814), "My Country 'Tis of Thee" (1831), "Dixie" (about 1859), "America the Beautiful" (1895), "Lift Every Voice and Sing" (1899), and "God Bless America" (1938).

What's so remarkable about America is that we're a nation based largely on ideals. What makes us one people is not our language, or our ethnicity, or our family backgrounds, or our religious creeds. Our essential unifying bond is a set of civic beliefs—which is why anyone can become an American. Our anthems reflect this astonishing fact.

The most celebrated ideal in these eight songs is freedom. All but one ("Dixie") stress it. We hail those "who fought and bled in freedom's cause." We sing of "a sweet land of liberty." Our voices "ring with the harmonics of Liberty." We go "walking that freedom highway." There are many other examples. According to our anthems, if America must be sung in one word, that word is freedom.

Yet two of these anthems link our nation to freedom's opposite. "We have come over a way that with tears have been watered/We have come, treading our path of the blood of the slaughtered." And "By the relief office I see my people/As they stood there hungry, I stood there asking/Is this land made for you and me?"

I'm glad that these hard sentences are in our anthems. I like living in a country big enough, and free enough, to include in its pantheon the painful truths told by James Weldon Johnson in his African American national anthem and by Woody Guthrie in his anthem of America's ignored and dispossessed. Our foundational songs tell us that American patriotism is more than mere celebration.

Four of these anthems praise America's natural beauty. I sing to America that "I love thy rocks and rills, thy woods and templed hills." God bless America "from the mountains to the prairies, to the oceans white with foam." America is beautiful "from sea to shining sea." That "golden valley" was made for you and me. What a huge, continent-sized country we live in—and how beautiful!

Most of our anthems invoke the divine. "In Heaven we place a manly trust, that truth and justice will prevail, and every scheme of bondage fail." We're a "heaven rescued land" whose "motto" is to trust God. We sing to "our fathers' God, Author of liberty." We pray that "shadowed beneath Thy hand, may we forever stand." And of course, we sing "God bless America, land that I love."

At the same time, like the theme of freedom, the theme of America's relationship to God comes in several flavors in these songs. Sometimes we're simply grateful for God's blessings. Sometimes we ask for divine protection and guidance. Sometimes, in my view, we come too close to suggesting that God especially favors America.

But sometimes, instead of believing that God today is on our side, we pray that tomorrow we can be a better people—perhaps more worthy of being on God's side. From "America the Beautiful": "America! America! God shed his grace on thee/Till selfish gain no longer stain the banner of the free!" And: "America! America! May God thy gold refine/Till all success be nobleness and every gain divine!" There is no complacency here, no confidence in our collective rectitude, only a challenge in the form of a prayer.

"America the Beautiful" is my favorite American anthem. It was written by Katherine Lee Bates—a professor of English literature at Wellesley College who likely had socialist political leanings—during a cross-country trip from Massachusetts to Colorado in the summer of 1893. It was her first trip west, and she clearly fell in love—as I did during my first extended trip west—with America's skies, mountains, prairies, and "waves of grain." She originally called her song "America," but to me the eventual popular title, "America the Beautiful," is even better.

Yet what I love most about this song is its confident hope that, with God's help, this remarkable American experiment in ordered liberty can make us better tomorrow than we are today. "America! America! God mend thine every flaw/Confirm thy soul in self-control, thy liberty in law!" My admiration for this song continues to grow.

SIGNS

"Sign": A display (such as a lettered board or a configuration of neon tubing) used to identify or advertise a place or product or viewpoint.

All signs reveal us.
—Eudora Welty

I love American signs and rise to praise them. I love the fact that they're everywhere, even where they don't belong. I love their astonishing variety, including their often pig-stomping vulgarity. I love the clamor and disorder of them. I love their incessant, usually unguided, syncretism. Most of all, I love the fact—well, at least it's my firm conviction—that looking at our signs is looking at us.

In his famous essay "The Power of the Powerless," Václav Havel invites us to consider the meaning of a shopkeeper in 1970s Communist-run Czechoslovakia putting up a sign in his store window saying, "Workers of the world, unite!" Havel asks: "What is he [the shopkeeper] trying to communicate to the world?" Does his sign reflect "any personal desire to acquaint the public with the ideal it expresses?" Havel doubts that it does. Instead, Havel concludes, the sign "contains a subliminal but very definite message" to his neighbors and his rulers:

> *I know what I must do. I behave in the manner expected of me. I can be depended upon and am beyond reproach. I am obedient and therefore have the right to be left in peace.*

In many unfree societies, signs put up by individuals serve this purpose, just as signs put up by the state serve the complementary purposes of glorifying rulers and reinforcing official ideology.

Not so much in the United States; indeed, more the opposite. American signs sing out eccentricity more than conformity, independence rather than obedience, and the right to engage all comers much more than the right to be left in peace. The subliminal message of American signs is not "I know what I must do"; it's rather, "Here's what I have to say!"

America's signs don't aim to placate our rulers or even our garden-variety local politicians, but rather to entice and persuade and provoke and plead with each other. The main flow of the communication is not vertical, but horizontal. That's why American signs are so insistent and also why they're everywhere. Our signs are *us*, as a form of visual-speak that never closes up for the night or goes on holiday. Our national experience strongly suggests that putting up an astonishing landscape of signs—small and large, elegant and garish, addressing everything from suntan lotion to salvation—is what people do if they are free to do it.

This reality has deeply shaped how America looks and feels, for both better and worse. For starters, consider what most of the world views as our crass commercialism. When I was a child, driving down long stretches of Mississippi and Alabama highways with my parents and brother, I remember the endless parade of "Stuckey's" billboards: *Stuckey's 100 miles! Stuckey's 90 miles! Stuckey's 80 miles!* ... and so on down the highway, almost trance-inducing, until we finally reached, well, Stuckey's. I've never much cared for what Stuckey's sold ("pecans candies gifts"), but to this day I'll pull into a Stuckey's anytime, in memory of those signs. Of course, as I look back, those yellow billboards also seem like a kind of unfolding roadside monstrosity—too big, too repetitive, maybe also too silly and wasteful.

But Americans tend to strive mightily for commercial success, so we accept and sometimes even admire brash, over-the-top salesmanship. We put up signs about everything, but by far the largest share concern buying and selling—and we make few if any apologies for it. Indeed, we seem to love this motto, reputed to be a Navy SEAL invention: "What's worth doing is worth overdoing, and at great expense." Many generations of foreign visitors, especially those from more settled and civilized societies, don't see it that way. They have noted and often criticized this part of who we are, but there it is. *Seventy miles!*

Another identity-revealing aspect of American signage is its aesthetic. Basically, there is none. Or perhaps more accurately, there is *every* aesthetic in our signage. Many of our signs are modern, polished, and beautifully crafted. Yet many—I'd guess most—are not in that tradition, which for me is terrific. I adore American signs that are distressed, careworn, and nearly played out. I'm also a sucker for homemade, jerry-rigged, and inelegant signs, including those with awkward or unusual wording. One of my favorites, for example, posted on the door of a wonderful Japanese eatery, says "No Outside Foods Allowed In."

Tom Wolfe once described Las Vegas as the only city in the world where buildings reflect the tastes of average citizens instead of sophisticated elites. The same is true regarding signage—but it's true almost everywhere in America, not just in Las Vegas. As a result, American signs don't shape us as much as they reveal and reflect us, especially at ground level and in our various aspects, warts and all. That's why chastising our American signs for their ordinariness and crassness—looking down on them from the heaven of good taste—is a bit like chastising waiters for the food we ordered.

The same is true with respect to American signs about religion and worldview. See one you don't agree with? Walk a little farther down the street. As a child in Mississippi, in those years a state in which prohibitionist belief was as strong as bootlegging was a booming business, I grew up with signs on cars and elsewhere saying, "For the sake of my family, I'll vote dry." Just recently I saw a sign in front of a fast-food restaurant near Clinton, Mississippi, saying, "Bring in Last Sunday's Church Bulletin for a 10 Percent Discount." These signs don't reflect my own way of making sense of the world. But I respect them, both on their own terms and as ways of understanding some of my fellow citizens.

And what about density? Is any nation on earth more densely signed than the United States? I doubt it. We paste signs on subway turnstiles. We put signs on our car bumpers and windows. We insinuate signs into airport baggage claim carousels, so we can watch them roll by along with our bags. We look up to the sky to notice airplane banners and blimps displaying signs. We put signs in our elevators and in our yards. Via teletron, they now dominate our sports stadiums. We festoon our highways with them, and often our streets and roads as well.

Myriad churches, gas stations, and one-off commercial roadside establishments have those rectangular displays—the ones with the plain black letters stuck on a white background—that change approximately weekly when weather permits, wanting to sell us not so much good stuff as good counsel: a verse from the Bible, a holy pun or perhaps a stern religious warning ("Christ or Chaos?"), a proverb ("Those Who Think They Can't Are Usually Right"), or just a kind thought. It's as though the folks who make up these signs want to talk to you personally but can't, so the sign is their way of getting a message in edgewise as you go rolling through their town.

When it pleases us, we promiscuously stack signs on top of each other and squish them together, as if any sign-free bit of space was at least in principle a wasted space. In America, it seems that anyone who owns or controls anything can put signs on it, and usually does. We like to speak out and be heard; quite often, it seems, we like to make a ruckus.

What unites us as Americans? Especially in this highly polarized era, in which our main feelings toward one another often seem to be anger and mistrust, what might we recognize as something we have in common? As modest and frail as this thought may seem—and I admit it's both—I want to suggest that we Americans have together made millions of signs telling us that we're a distinctive people.

The fundamental American idea is freedom. The fundamental way Americans aspire to live together, established at the founding and stated in our motto, is *E pluribus unum*—from many, one. But to comprehend this way of life you don't have to read the history books or memorize the sacred civic phrases. You just have to look around. Every day you'll see millions of us, in great variety and discord, brashly singing out to one another in our signs, as free American citizens.

SHORT MAN RECREATION
Enjoy
Coca-Cola

O'Charley's
JOIN
US
FREE PIE
WEDNESDAY

bôilicious44
Vietnamese To Go
44 Street
UNISEX SALON
&
BARBERSHOP
212-867-0875
166 East 44 Street
SHOE REPAIR
WATCH REPAIR
KEYS MADE
168 E 44 Street
212-490-2874
Smart
DevicePro
Professional Care For Your Smart Devices
PHONES • TABLETS • LAPTOPS • MAC'S
347-759-8317
ww.SmartDevicePro.com
168 E 44 Street

CHAMPAGNE
MONTAUDON
MARGARITA
BLACK
LIVES
MATTER

King George
Termite & Pest
775-0000

FOOD
OKAY

CHEAP CIGS-COLD BEER-LIQUOR
$36.13
$39.95
WOLF
MAVERICK
GREAT VALUE
$34.89
$43.38
DOMINATOR
FIREWORKS
JAMESON

BERRY'S BAR B QUE
CHICKEN AND RIBS
BENTON, MS

KEEP
AMERICA
SECULAR
CONNECTICUT
VALLEY
ATHEISTS
CVATHEISTS.org

"Fight Crime, Shoot Back"
J & S GUN DEPOT
Easley, SC
(864) 859-9065

piggly
wiggly
CHUCK ROAST $379 LB
TURKEY NECKS 79 LB

HOT SANDWIC
BONNIE-BLUE
"Oh boy - what a meal"

PIE

BEST CHINESE
GIFT CARDS
CARRY OUT
EVENTS & CATERING

WE NEED
GRILLMAN 16 HR
MON TUE WED TH FR SAT SUN
Off 6 Am - 2 Pm 3 Pm 10 Pm 3 Pm - 10 Pm 3 Pm - 10 Pm 3 Pm - 10 Pm 3 Pm - 10 Pm
Olso we need
DISHWASERS

Antioch BAPTIST CHURCH
Available Services:
MARRIAGES PERFORMED
CATERING FOR ALL OCCASIONS
BANQUETS · CHARTERED BUSES
FUNERAL ARRANGEMENTS.....

OUR
LITTLE BABE

GONE TO THE TOTE-SUM

All my life I've called convenience stores "Tote-Sums." As in, "He's gone to the Tote-Sum," or "Let's stop at the Tote-Sum and get some beer." Moreover, it seems that nearly everyone over the age of 40 who grew up, as I did, in Jackson, Mississippi, tends to refer to any convenience store as "the Tote-Sum."

Martin Cooper, who runs a Facebook page called "Memories of Growing Up in Jackson, Mississippi," says that "Tote-Sum stores come up frequently on the site" and that "just about everybody I know who grew up with them continues to call all convenience stores Tote-Sum stores." This hardy linguistic group includes many Jacksonians who, like me, left Jackson years ago, but who continue regularly and un-self-consciously to use the term, despite the fact that, when we do, we usually get quizzical stares.

Why do we do it? This question interests me. In a time when so much in our public life seems to divide and anger us, perhaps it's worth reflecting on those remaining things, even long-past things, which can unite and soothe us. So let us now remember—or more precisely, let us now examine the meaning of remembering—some convenience stores called Tote-Sums.

> *Ed had three daughters . . . When the girls were young Ed took them out each Sunday in his Austin Healy to Seale-Lily Ice Cream parlor, the Tote-Sum, and an amusement park featuring a super slide.*
>
> —Obituary of James E. Ruff, Jr. of Jackson, Mississippi, *Northside Sun*, 2016

The Tote-Sum to which Ed Ruff took his daughters on Sundays, across the street from Seale-Lily Ice Cream, was about a half-mile from the house I grew up in, and the first commercial establishment to which I was allowed to walk on my own. Starting at age seven, with my weekly "allowance" of 25 cents in my pocket, I'd walk up to the Tote-Sum on most Saturdays, usually hoping to buy the latest Superman comic book, which would set me back 12 cents, and also (if my budget allowed) a large Coca-Cola Icee, a slushy carbonated drink wildly popular at that time with the elementary school crowd.

Several years later, at the same Tote-Sum, I'd sneak past the comic books in favor of visiting the "adult" magazine rack in the rear of the store, near the back exit and mostly out of sight of the cashier, where at my leisure I could study the photos of scantily clad women (or glaciers if anyone looked my way) in *National Geographic* and in the risqué magazines.

My first Tote-Sum, officially known as Tote-Sum Store No. 2, circa 1960s. Photo by Deborah Hill Harloe.

When I was 10, I often rode my bike to another Tote-Sum, perhaps a mile away, in search of baseball cards, candy, or whatever else I could afford. My frequent companion on these treks was my dog, MacArthur. One day MacArthur took a Tastykake from a shelf and ate it on the spot without notifying me or the guy behind the counter. I had already spent all the money I had, so we skulked away, with only MacArthur in a good mood. When we got home and I told my mother, she gave me a quarter and insisted that we go back to pay the man for the Tastykake, which we did. Later that day, MacArthur was hit by a car in front of our house and died. (For some reason we let our dogs run free in those days, despite the dangers.) For years afterward, whenever my family remembered MacArthur, we took some comfort in the fact that his final meal, which he'd thoroughly enjoyed, came from the Tote-Sum.

In sixth grade, I was a safety "patrol boy," stationed each morning and afternoon at a traffic intersection near my elementary school, charged with helping the younger children cross the street. Near that intersection was a Tote-Sum, where I breakfasted each school morning throughout that school year, enjoying a Mountain Dew soft drink and a pre-packaged Honey Bun, purchased with money given to me by my father for just that purpose. To me it was a fine time and good eating.

I don't think my Tote-Sum experiences were unusual. Here are some comments from a recent discussion of Tote-Sums on a Facebook page called "Northeast Jackson Remembered":

> *I think we went to the tote-sum every day! The one we went to was where Green Oak is now, and you would just drive up and they would come out and bring you what you asked for. My brother worked at a Tote-Sum store as a car runner in the late 1950s. The folks who ran it got all the boys started smoking. My brother was a smoker all his life and my mom was furious that they got him started.*

> *I worked at a Tote-Sum part time after school and on weekends, I'm thinking maybe 1955, '56, '57. It was awhile back, but it was a great experience. Those stores gave me a*

lesson in work habits and how to treat customers that I used my whole work life.

Will never forget how good those Coca-Cola Icees tasted on a hot summer day, and the best part is we could walk there by ourselves. My children and now their children will never know that kind of freedom.

We rode our bikes there all the time. Icees and Pac-Man!

In the summer I would walk down to the Tote-Sum and buy a Grapette and a bag of peanuts. I remember the first time I heard the phrase "convenience store" and I thought to myself, "Tote-Sum is so much more convenient to say."

It was the Road of Remembrance, where the very first one opened up at. Later it got to be a dangerous place.

Whence came Tote-Sums? The principal founders were Charles S. Barry, Jr., a native of Dallas, Texas, who was born in 1912 and moved to Jackson in 1948, and two brothers, Joe and James Wood, also from Dallas. Opening a convenience store in Jackson, said Charles Barry's son Bryan many years later, "just looked like something they wanted to try."

These men would also certainly have been familiar with a chain of Dallas convenience stores called "Tote'm Stores," which date back to 1927 and probably constitute the nation's first convenience store chain. They were originally called Southland Ice Stores, but in the late 1920s the owners began putting Alaskan-type totem poles in front of the stores, which many customers liked, and which therefore caused the owners to change the name—you may have to be Southern to follow the logic here—to "Tote'm Stores." As in, where you see totem poles, and also where you buy things to tote home. At any rate, there were 60 Tote'm Stores in the Dallas area by 1939. Then came another name change. In 1946, seeking to emphasize their convenient-for-the-customer operating hours, the Tote'm Stores changed their name to "7-Eleven," and the rest, as they say, is history.

A Tote'm Store in Dallas, Texas, circa 1930s. Photo courtesy of 7-Eleven, Inc.

Meanwhile in Jackson, the three transplanted Texans opened the first (slightly altered from "Tote'm") Tote-Sum Store in early 1949, on Road of Remembrance in west Jackson, when Jackson was a city of about 100,000 residents. Later that year, the men opened Tote-Sum Store No. 2 (see photo above) in north Jackson.

In 1952, there were three Tote-Sums. In 1956, there were six. In 1965, there were 10. By the early 1970s, when Jackson had about

154,000 residents, there would be 21. In 1984, when the Tote-Sum chain was sold to Junior Food Stores, based in Meridian, Mississippi, thus bringing an end to a 35-year run as a locally owned chain, there were 13 Tote-Sums in Jackson.

I don't think Tote-Sums were unusual. In *Field of Dreams*, a terrific 1989 movie about memory, magic, and baseball, we learn about "Doc" Graham, for decades a beloved figure in his hometown of Chisholm, Minnesota.

> *Ray: Well, he sounds like he was a wonderful man.*
> *Terry: Half the towns in North America have a "Doc" Graham.*

That's how I feel about Tote-Sums. I'm sure that hundreds of American towns have had locally owned stores that people identify with and remember with great fondness.

Yet *why* such identification? Why such fondness? After all, at one level, they're just stores! They're quotidian. We go there to buy things. But on another level, there appears to be something about them, or at least about our memories of them, that brings us together and creates a sense of community based on shared public experiences.

The great writer Eudora Welty, a native of Jackson, writes lovingly about what people who, like her, grew up in Jackson in the 1910s and 1920s called "corner stores" or "neighborhood stores." Located in urban neighborhoods, these forerunners of what after World War II came to be called "convenience stores" catered to local residents who wanted to make quick, usually small purchases of groceries without having to travel all the way to the central business district (or in later years, to the shopping center). Welty says that going to the corner store as a child meant that her world became more exciting and dazzling, and she remembers that "enchantment is cast upon you by all those things you weren't supposed to have need for . . ."

Going to the store to buy something for her mother (and then keeping and spending the change) also meant a burst of freedom:

> *The happiness of errands was in part that of running for the moment away from home, a free spirit. I believed the Little Store to be a center of the outside world, and hence of happiness . . .*

Decades later, the novelist and my high school classmate Mary Ann Rodman similarly described for her generation a child's happiness in venturing to the store: "Mississippi in March was for shorts and azaleas and biking to the Tote-Sum for ICEEs."

Like the corner store—and also like the 17th-century British invention, the coffeehouse—the modern convenience store is a part-private, part-public space in which people who don't know each other, or don't know each other well, can mingle together on easy terms. It's also a known institution of civil society—even Jacksonians who never, or rarely, went to the Tote-Sum knew about the Tote-Sum.

Tote-Sums certainly became a fixture in many spheres of Jackson's public life. As early as 1950, Tote-Sum was sponsoring a Ladies' Bowling League team in Jackson. For decades the chain sponsored one of the city's Little League baseball teams. I remember as a Little Leaguer myself in the 1960s playing each summer against the boys proudly wearing the words "Tote-Sum Stores" on their uniforms, and I remember reading stories in the local newspapers such as this one, from 1975: "Tote-Sum Stores defeated Colonial Baking Saturday night 11 to 3 to bring the two teams within one game of each other going into the final week of play."

Over the years Tote-Sums became thoroughly insinuated into the city's visual and civic landscape. So when public "streaking" made perhaps its first appearance in Jackson, in 1976, it surprised few Jacksonians that it would occur at a Tote-Sum. In this case, a city police officer, J.W. Willoughby, was at a Tote-Sum when, as the police department later reported, a girl "came in and asked for a can of Coca-Cola," whereupon Officer Willoughby "looked around" and "noticed the girl had no clothes on." The girl then "fled the store, but was caught by Willoughby in the middle of Jefferson Street."

Driving around Jackson, you'd encounter tall (44 feet high!) signs made of neon lights blinking "TOTE-SUM" on and off. The chain's billboard and print media advertisements—including "Tote Sum of Everything" and "Tote-Sum Stores were made in Mississippi"—were hard to miss.

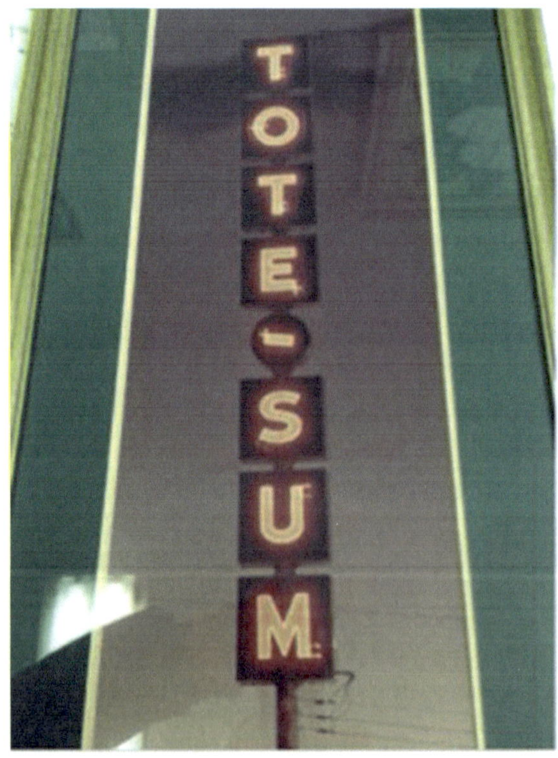

The famous Tote-Sum sign, circa early 1980s. Photo courtesy of Temple W. Barry.

In 1981, if you wanted to pre-register for a "Turkey Shoot" sponsored by the Jackson Police and the Jackson Parks and Recreation Department, you could do so (the entry fee was $3) at any Tote-Sum. In 1983, if you wanted to watch the first 3-D movie (*Gorillas at Large*) ever broadcast on a Mississippi television station, you could get special 3-D glasses at any Tote-Sum.

Many Jacksonians worked at the Tote-Sum over the years. In particular, hundreds and perhaps thousands of Jackson teenagers worked part-time at the Tote-Sum, either after school or at night or on weekends. For many, it was their first job. In 1977, when an 18-year-old boy from the public high school I'd attended was shot to death during a robbery attempt at the Tote-Sum where he was working after school, Charles Barry, the president and co-founder of Tote-Sum, said, "We'd watched him grow up."

In *Field of Dreams*, someone says that people re-experiencing a game they loved as children feel like "they've been dipped in magic waters." I'm not sure that people recalling a store from their childhood, even if that store is the Tote-Sum, feel that way. But perhaps they do, at least some of them, at least a bit. I confess that I do.

In 1861, Abraham Lincoln in his First Inaugural Address spoke to a country on the verge of civil war. Trying to describe what it is—what we have—that might yet have the power to dissipate rancor and reduce mistrust, the new president cited only "the mystic chords of memory."

I've long viewed that phrase mainly as a hard-to-understand piece of poetry, but perhaps Lincoln is simply saying as concisely as he can what he believes is true. When public life grows coarse and ugly, and we seem increasingly to view each other as strangers, perhaps it's not shared political values that can keep us together.

Or a shared religion. Or a common race. Or shared levels of education and affluence. Or common dreams for the future. Perhaps more than these, what truly has the power to keep us together in divisive times are the mystic chords of memory—what we find that we can remember together, even seemingly small things, of life and time and place.

“BETTER ANGELS”: NOTES ON A PHRASE

Across our broad land, there’s a new birth of enthusiasm for the phrase “better angels.” At least three nonprofit organizations are now called “Better Angels.” Two best-selling books from the 2010s, along with numerous others that weren’t best-sellers, feature the phrase in their titles. Two recent documentary films are called *Better Angels*. So is a 2019 song recorded by Barbra Streisand as well as a 2019 album and concert tour by two other recording artists. I’ve seen the phrase used as both a corporate slogan and as names of conferences. God help us, there’s now a beer called “Better Angels.” In our politics, members from both sides of the aisle seem increasingly to invoke the phrase.

For the source of this trend, we can look generally to the ugliness of our current public conversation. The more our better angels flee us, the more we discuss them and wish for their return. And of course we can look particularly to Abraham Lincoln, who used the phrase so beautifully in his First Inaugural Address on March 4, 1861, on the eve of our Civil War.

> *I am loath to close. We are not enemies, but friends. We must not be enemies. Though passion may have strained, it must not break our bonds of affection. The mystic chords of memory, stretching from every battle-field and patriot grave to every living heart and hearth-stone, all over this broad land, will yet swell the chorus of the Union, when again touched, as surely they will be, by the better angels of our nature.*

Although Lincoln's peroration is justly famous, Lincoln did not coin the phrase "better angels." The phrase and its cognates have appeared in English literature since at least the early 17th century. To understand the phrase, and to deepen our understanding of Lincoln and his times, let's examine the lineage and usages of this evocative term.

We know that Lincoln personally wrote the phrase into his speech. We even have a picture of it. We also know that William Seward, who would serve as Lincoln's Secretary of State and arguably his most important advisor, had originally suggested that Lincoln close his speech by calling upon "the guardian angel of the nation"—a pietistic but stock phrase that would surely have been little noted and not long remembered.

But Lincoln scratched out Seward's suggestion and replaced it in his own handwriting with a phrase saying that what the nation needed in its time of reckoning would not come from outside us, as in an angel guarding us from above, but instead from within us—something "better" in the "nature" of both Northerners and Southerners. In stating so poetically that profound idea, Lincoln in one phrase told us as much as any president before or since who we can be, and thus what America is.

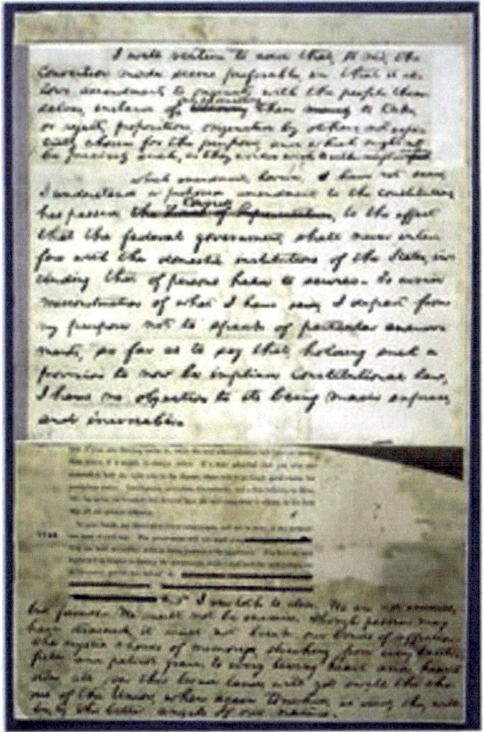

The final page of Lincoln's First Inaugural Address, with the concluding paragraph written by hand. Library of Congress.

No one knows with certainty how Lincoln first encountered the phrase "better angels." But based on available evidence, one possible source stands out as the most likely: William Shakespeare's play *Othello,* written about 1603. In the play, Othello has murdered his wife, Desdemona, accusing her of adultery. Her uncle, Gratiano, declares that it's good that Desdemona's father, Brabantio, is dead:

Poor Desdemona! I am glad thy father's dead:
Thy match was mortal to him, and pure grief
Shore his old thread in twain: did he live now,

This sight would make him do a desperate turn,
Yea, curse his better angel from his side,
And fall to reprobation.

Three factors point to *Othello* as Lincoln's source. It's highly likely that Lincoln read the play. There's no positive evidence that he read any of the other English works published prior to 1861 that use the phrase. And as regards intended meaning, Lincoln uses the term exactly the way Shakespeare uses it.

For Shakespeare, as for Lincoln, "better angels" were neither individual people nor supernatural beings, but instead aspects of temperament. A "better angel," in this construal, is a composite of those praiseworthy traits within us that exist alongside, and contest with, unworthy traits. In *Othello*, for example, we fear that Brabantio, in his "pure grief" at his daughter's murder, would "curse his better angel from his side" such that he would do deeds of "desperate turn," causing him to be damned by God ("fall to reprobation"). In one of his sonnets, written about 1599, Shakespeare similarly tells us of "two spirits" that are "both from me"—a "better angel" that is "right fair" and a "worser spirit" that "tempteth my better angel from my side" and thus "would corrupt my saint to be a devil."

For Lincoln, the "better angels of our nature" are those civic and patriotic qualities, shaped by shared memory, that permit us, even in times of national fracturing, to "swell the chorus of the Union." This conception of "better angels" as admirable aspects of temperament, or aspirations toward what is good, is likely the dominant meaning of the term in English and U.S. history.

Edward Bulwer-Lytton in about 1839, for example, prefigures Lincoln exactly when he yearns for "the better angels of the human heart." Earlier, in 1715, in Nicholas Rowe's *The Tragedy of Lady Jane Gray,* we learned that we need "our better Angels" to help us participate in "Friendship's Hour and Friendship's Office":

To come when Counsel and when Help [for others] is wanting,
To share the Pain of every gnawing Care,
To speak of Comfort in the Time of Trouble,
To reach a Hand and save thee from Adversity.

What are the "worser spirits" that our "better angels" strive to overcome? An essayist in *The London Magazine* in 1784 says:

Away then, fear, despondency, and doubt,
My better angels drive such traitors out.

A British essayist in 1832 tells a tale:

As he at once formed his decision to obey his better angel, his spirit, previously clogged by the dull, heavy weights of combined misery and despair, seemed now of ethereal lightness and buoyancy.

In *The Golden Farmer*, from about 1832, Benjamin Webster says:

You've proved my better angels. Ere I knew yon, ay, and since, for a time, the vice of gain, either by honest or dishonest means, had taken possession of my breast to an almost miserly feeling; but your bright example has taught my heart to flow with better thoughts.

In a sermon from 1837, the Rev. William Whewell warns his congregation:

We not only refuse to listen to our better angel, but drive him from us with mocks and insults. We plunge willingly into the slough of selfishness, and refuse to pass onwards.

In 1851, the Rev. Frederic D. Huntington preached a sermon in Cambridge, Massachusetts, following the passage of the Fugitive

Slave Act—a federal law that the anti-slavery Huntington fervently opposed, and which Lincoln, notwithstanding his opposition to slavery, supported in his Inaugural Address as a means of attempting to preserve the Union. Calling the law a "national sin," Huntington warns of what he calls "the everlasting law":

> *With every wanton denial of our purer aspirations, those aspirations themselves grow faint. Resistance to our better angels drives those angels away.*

(While there's no evidence to prove it, it's certainly plausible to suspect that Lincoln might have read this sermon.)

If this small corpus is to be trusted, our "better angels" as evoked in our literature are primarily those inner traits guiding us toward friendship, unity, good conscience, and lightness and buoyancy of spirit, as they are simultaneously challenged and sometimes overcome by tendencies toward selfishness, divisiveness, fear, despondency, and heaviness and dullness of spirit.

This conception of "better angels" has continued into the present. Here is the Rev. Patrick Conroy, the chaplain of the U.S. House of Representatives, in July 2019:

> *If you are a person of faith, ultimately everything in our lives, our communities and our culture is a battle between darker spirits and our better angels.*

There are exceptions to this usage. Sometimes in our literature a "better angel" is a person, usually a woman. The poet and dramatist Henry Jones in 1753 describes his "gracious Queen" as "My better Angel, and my Guardian Genius!" A poet in London in 1761 says: "WIVES our better angels are." And lest we forget daughters, here is William Guthrie in 1754:

Daughters, said he, thou hast acted like my better Angel. Henceforth I resign myself to your Conduct.

Sometimes a "better angel" is, well, an angel. The historian Francis Newman in 1878 describes early Jewish proselytism:

Special angels, perhaps evil spirits, were supposed to uphold the pagan dynasties, which fell when the invisible patron was overcome by better angels.

But "better angels" as either individuals or as supernatural beings appear to be less common. The dominant conception, at least through 1861, and as clearly intended by Lincoln, is captured precisely by Charles Dickens in his 1841 novel, *Barnaby Rudge*:

So do the shadows of our own desires stand between us and our better angels, and thus their brightness is eclipsed.

For Lincoln, the "shadows of our desires" standing in 1861 between "us" and "our better angels" were fanaticism, fear, self-righteousness, and perhaps most of all, mistrust.

Nearly his entire address that day was an appeal for the restoration of trust. He speaks directly to Southerners, seeking to reassure them that the government will not threaten their peace, property, or personal security. He insists that as president he cannot legally interfere with slavery in the Southern states and has no desire to do so even if he could. He reiterates his support of the Fugitive Slave Law. He does refuse, as did most Republicans, and to the alarm of white Southerners, to accept the Supreme Court's pro-slavery *Dred Scott* decision as final, but even here Lincoln equivocates and avoids strong language. The tone throughout, according to the respected Lincoln scholars J. G. Randall and David Herbert Donald, "struck the note of gentle firmness and breathed the spirit of conciliation and of friendliness to the South."

Citing law and history, Lincoln argues that the Union is perpetual, cannot consent to its own destruction, and therefore cannot be legally undone on the "mere motion" of one or a group of states. He says that, as a president sworn to uphold the law, he has no legal authority under the Constitution to "fix terms for the separation of the States." He says that he trusts that this fact "will not be regarded as a menace" and that in carrying out his "simple duty" to defend and maintain the Union "there needs to be no bloodshed or violence, and there shall be none unless it is forced upon the national authority."

Like a lawyer speaking to a jury, he suggests that separation would make the nation's current problems worse, not better. He appeals to reason: "Physically speaking, we cannot separate." He proposes that in a democracy the ultimate wisdom of the people can be trusted to prevail, and he reminds those who would oppose his Administration that even bad governments have limited powers and limited terms of office. He says that both North and South "profess to be content with the Union, if all constitutional rights can be maintained," and pledges again that these rights will be maintained. He pleads for calmness. He argues against a rush to action: "Nothing valuable can be lost by taking time." He closes by appealing to "our bonds of affection" rooted in "the mystic chords of memory." And finally, he promises that we will be "again touched" by "the better angels of our nature."

In practical terms, the speech was a failure in nearly every respect. Hardly a Southerner attended the inauguration ceremonies. Many Southern newspapers, especially in the Deep South, simply ignored Lincoln's address, and those that did notice the speech frequently mangled and misrepresented the text in their coverage. Southern commentators commonly portrayed Lincoln as an untrustworthy hypocrite, claiming in the speech that he did not want civil war while promising in the same speech to do exactly what would cause one. As an editorial in the Midgeville, Georgia, *Southern Federal Union* put it: "Mr. Lincoln talks with a forked tongue." On Inauguration Day the *Richmond Examiner* called Lincoln "a beastly figure" whom "no one can hear with patience or look on without disgust," and the following day the *Richmond Enquirer* said that Lincoln's address consisted of "the deliberate language of the fanatic."

Lincoln took office as a beleaguered president, widely disliked and mistrusted in the country. Many in his own party viewed him as a crude, unreliable man. Many in the South viewed him as a would-be despot, while many others in all parts of the country viewed him as a weakling who would be, or could be, controlled by others. The immediate result of his election was to further divide an already dangerously divided nation. His Inaugural Address did little to change any of these realities. Five weeks after the speech, Confederate forces fired upon Fort Sumter, South Carolina, and the war came.

The year 1861 was an important year for a phrase we now remember and revere. It was not a good year, at least insofar as Lincoln intended the term, for the better angels of our nature.

ACKNOWLEDGMENTS

Although I've revised and updated these essays, all of them except Chapter 1 were originally published in either *The American Interest* or the *Deseret News*. Chapter 1 was originally published in *USA Today*. I'm grateful to the editors of these publications.

All shortcomings herein are my own, as the required and true-enough saying goes, but I've also benefited greatly from sharing drafts and discussing many of these issues over time with a number of friends and colleagues, including Marie Antoon, Hunter Baker, William J. Doherty, Paul Edwards, Adam Garfinkle, David Lapp, April Lawson, Kathleen R. McGowen, Donna Murphy, Ciaran O'Connor, Jonathan Rauch, Raina Sacks, Timothy J. Shaffer, Peter Skerry, Charles Reagan Wilson, and John Wood, Jr.

In the introduction to his book *Modernity on Endless Trial*, Leszek Kolakowski, one of the great minds of his generation, says that his book contains no new ideas. Kolakowski was not modest. He was honest. Every serious idea you or I might express, rough-hew them how we will, comes from other people, usually quite a few of them. For me in this regard, there are far more than I can count. But I'll start and end with my wife, Raina Sacks; our children, Raymond, Alexandra, and Sophia; and my parents, Diane and Dave Blankenhorn.

About Braver Angels

Please know how grateful I feel to be a part of Braver Angels. I am amazed at everyone's sincerity, enthusiasm, collegiality, and commitment to the mission. Braver Angels is doing such amazing and important work in our country and it is a huge source of hope for me and so many others.
—Braver Angels leader Susie Hodges, San Mateo, California

The work you are doing may just save us as a democratic culture.
—Terry Roberts, National Paideia Center

Braver Angels is doing some of the most important work today to restore and repair our democracy.
—Jonathan Haidt, author of *The Righteous Mind*

733 Third Avenue, 16th Floor
New York, NY 10017
www.braverangels.org
212.246.3942

Made in United States
Troutdale, OR
02/19/2025

29113181R00086